STRIVING

TO MAKE IT

MY HOME

Books by Marion Starkey

STRIVING
TO MAKE IT
MY HOME

The Story of
AMERICANS FROM AFRICA

MARION L. STARKEY

W · W · NORTON & COMPANY · INC · New York

For Max and Marion MacLean

IN MEMORY OF VITAL YEARS
AT HAMPTON INSTITUTE

CONTENTS

FOREWORD

THE QUEST that this book represents began somewhat before Pearl Harbor in a bull session at Hampton Institute, Virginia. It happened in an English class; somehow the formal business on the agenda, maybe the case of pronouns, maybe the inner meaning of a Shakespearean sonnet, had exploded into a discussion of Race.

Such a diversion was to be expected periodically, especially in a course like English, where no topic is irrelevant. In those days actions like lunch counter sit-ins and freedom rides had not been thought of; the only outlet the students had when social inequities pressed them too hard was discussion. These were Negro students in a college with an interracial faculty; some got through life placidly, shrugging their shoulders at racial barriers as just one more of the troublesome Facts of Life; but others, powerfully aware that though they were as American as Huck Finn and johnny-cake, they were not so accepted, perennially let their sense of injustice explode into expression. When it happened, the only thing to do was to let the case of pronouns and Shakespeare's sonnets ride while they had their say.

What precipitated this particular discussion I have no idea. What I do remember is the response to a question I presently raised.

"Suppose we could turn the clock back three hundred years," I said. "Suppose we could wipe out the whole history of the slave trade. Then your ancestors need never have come to America, and you would still be Africans. Would you rather have had it that way?"

There was dead silence, then a murmur, then a roar: "No!"

It was not a reasoned response. What did these young people—or I—know of Africa? There were then no visible surges toward African nationalism or Pan-Africanism; they knew no more of their remote motherland than current clichés and their random contacts with a handful of fellow students from Liberia, Sierra Leone, and what was still called the Gold Coast. Their response accordingly was not only unreasoned but in some respects unreasonable; but it was spontaneous and it was real: they proclaimed themselves Americans.

And I have teased myself ever since with these questions. What was the human reality of their ancestral story? What was the way of life from which the Africans came? What were the stages of their transition to life in the new world? By what social alchemy did Africans become Americans? This book is my attempt to find the answers.

The difficult query concerns the human reality of the story, especially in its subjective aspects. The objective facts are well known. Two massive documentary collections, Elizabeth Donnan's *Documents of the Slave Trade*, and Helen T. Catterall's *Judicial Cases Concerning Slavery*, give an enormously detailed account of the mechanics of the involuntary immigration. But all such records were set down by white men, traders on both sides of the Atlantic, captains, super-cargoes, to whom the immigrants were so much merchandise of a particularly difficult and perishable nature. Where are the records of the immigrants themselves?

There are a few. When the abolition movement became active in America, "autobiographies" were published of American Negroes who remembered what their African parents had told them. But for good reason second genera-tion Afro-Americans found it difficult to grasp the living reality of the experience; moreover, the stories were usually ghost-written by white people who obscured what reality may have survived by their own sentimental preoccupations. One hears of innocent African children snatched by brutal white men while they walked hand in hand by the seashore, or a whole family shanghaied when they boarded a slaver to go sightseeing. When, very rarely, some such incidents occurred they represented a mode of enslavement that went out with Prince Henry the Navigator and Sir John Hawkins, neither of whom made a direct contribution to America's most peculiar institution.

The authentic memoirs can almost be counted on one's thumbs. One is by the boy of Benin who took the name of Gustavus Vassa. His story of his capture in 1756, his trans-portation to America, his first days in Barbados and Virginia, is the best there is. Eventually he became an Englishman, and of all things, a polar explorer, which rather removes him from the main body of this story. Nevertheless much of his narrative is important, and I have centered four of my chap-ters on his adventures: "Boy of Benin," "Immigrant Ship," "Marketplace," "The Freedmen." Thereafter he has a way of bobbing up in unexpected contexts. Unusual as his total ex-perience was, factors in it illuminate nearly every phase of the Afro-American story.

Another original narrative is that of the Connecticut patriarch, Venture Smith. Apparently he did not write his own story, but it was faithfully set down in 1837 and has the ring of truth. It is less subjective than Vassa's, for Smith was a phlegmatic character, and he too, because he lived in the North, is atypical. But his is the only narrative of an Afro-American that comprises a second and even a third generation.

In writing I have tried to answer in sequence the questions with which my inquiry began. For a picture of the African way of life I have relied on the voyages of Mungo Park. This does some violence to chronology, since the young Scot reached Africa in 1795 in the waning days of the American slave trade, but that I think is unimportant. Whereas earlier narratives deal with the gaudy life at the royal courts of Abomey and Benin, Park's tells about the intimacies of life in that timeless, most enduring of institutions, the African village. While in Africa Park became in effect an African, even to the extent of journeying to the coast in a slave coffle.

Next, though it took place half a century earlier, comes Vassa's boyhood in Benin, his kidnapping and transportation on a slave ship. To give objectivity to his account of the Middle Passage, I have blended his story with that of the voyage of Captain John Newton on the *Duke of Argyle*. Then in the chapter called "Marketplace," I follow Vassa to Virginia and England.

The chapter entitled "The Seasoning" was the most difficult to write. Sociologists and historians dismiss the vital period of the African's adjustment to America as "preconscious history," putting the reconstruction of the experience on a par with an adult's capacity to recall his infantile experience through the birth canal. Except for Vassa's it is indeed impossible to find one consecutive, individual story, but wonders can be done by piecing together bits of information. The most illuminating account I found was in the records of a kind of "senate investigating committee" of the time. This was an inquiry into West Indian slavery made by the British

House of Lords, before Parliament imposed abolition on the colonies. These records contain extraordinary material, completely untouched, as far as I know, by other historians.

Later in the story I have supplemented them with a detailed account of the remarkable incident known as Vesey's Rebellion. Here my interest lies in the picture of South Carolina, where American slavery took what might be called its classic form. I have also tried to show in this section the evolving status of the free man of color, and the virile part played by Africans imported in the last days of the legal slave trade.

For a description of the social alchemy by which Africans became conscious Americans, I have centered on the free Negro community of Philadelphia, from its dramatic part in the yellow fever epidemic of 1793, its rejection of the American Colonization Society's proposal that it return *en masse* to the African "homeland," to the beginning of its long, long fight for recognition of its people as American citizens.

All this is a story commonly looked back upon with guilt and shame, what one psychologist calls the "uncanny emotions." Gunnar Myrdal, the Swedish sociologist, who achieved in his *An American Dilemma* a near definitive study of Negro-white relationships, has expressed the theory that the "moral lag" in the application of American ideals of equality to the Negro has burdened the nation with a collective sense of guilt. It is also true that some Negroes are reluctant to look to a past that includes bondage. But the shame was not the bondsman's; and as for the guilt—though obviously we have paid for the sins of our fathers well past the second and third generations—the weight thereof should depend not on the irrevocable past but on how we go on. It may be that at long last we shall go on well.

ACKNOWLEDGMENTS

Research on this book involved highly enjoyable travel. Thanks to the Guggenheim Foundation I was able to get to West Africa, the object there being not formal research but to get my own personal impression of peoples and backgrounds.

My intensive research was done at the South Carolina Historical Society in Charleston, where Mrs. Mary Prior was helpful and hospitable; the South Carolina State Archives in Columbia; The Virginia Archives in Richmond; the Negro History Collection at Hampton Institute, Virginia; the manuscript room of the Library of Congress; the Pennsylvania Historical Society in Philadelphia; the Schonberg Collection of the New York Public Library. Aside from these visits the bulk of my research was carried on at the Boston Athenaeum and the Widener Library at Harvard.

Among the many to whom I owe a debt of gratitude are Dr. Gordon W. Allport of Harvard, Mrs. Huldah Blackmer of the Saugus Public Library, Mr. Claude C. Dennis of Monrovia, Liberia, Miss Margaret Hackett of the Boston Athenaeum, Mr. Edward A. Laycock of the *Boston Globe*, Mrs. Barbara Morse of Saugus, Dr. Howard Thurman of Boston University, Mrs. Francis Irons of Montpelier, Vermont.

STRIVING

TO MAKE IT

MY HOME

CHAPTER ONE

INVITATION
TO AMERICA

Whoever goes beyond the charted limits of the earth's surface must be prepared to encounter chimeras. The voyager is duly forewarned by sketches on his charts where the blank spaces beyond the realistic contours of land and inlet are dotted with mermaids and monsters.

Accordingly the first mariners to venture down the West African coast since the Carthaginians of antiquity (who mindful of their monopoly of trade were responsible for some of the chimeras) were not unduly surprised to observe a covy of sea monsters near Arguin, off Cape Blanco. There were about two dozen of them; they appeared to be monstrous seabirds that propelled themselves through the water with multiple feet.

When the Portuguese drew nearer and saw the myth resolve into dark-skinned men paddling their canoes, they were not disappointed. Here was something more valuable than

zoological specimens to be shipped back to Portugal; here
was booty. Though the West African coast was new to the
Europeans, the West Africans were not; those who lived in
the interior had sometimes been captured by the Moors and
conveyed across the Sahara to be sold in Europe as slaves.
Divine Providence had created them for this purpose; their
color was the mark of Cain, whom the historian of this expedition identified as a son of Noah.

Joyfully the Portuguese fell upon the naked fishermen and
transferred to their caravel all it would hold, about fourteen
men. Some struggled in the water until they drowned; others
got their canoes away to spread the alarm. It was regret-
table, but it couldn't be helped. And so in 1443 began the
first direct enslavement of the West Africans, the earliest
beginning of the slave trade.

Compared to what came later, it was a harmless beginning. For one thing, Portuguese priests saw the captives as
men with souls to save. An injunction was laid upon Prince
Henry the Navigator, organizer of these expeditions, to bring
the true faith to these people; and when captives were up-
rooted in far greater numbers, farther down the coast from
the Lagos area, Portuguese convents received the orphans
and gave them a Christian education, seminaries accepted
dark-skinned candidates for the priesthood, and even under
duress the adult African laborers were recognized not as
beasts of burden but as men.

Besides, the trade was on a small scale, even when as many
as 800 slaves were imported in a peak year. That so many
were taken was due to the fact that after the expulsion of
the Moors both Spain and Portugal had more land to till
than they had laborers to till it. But there were limits to this
land, and all things being equal, the trade might have run
its course without any profound effect on Africa or Europe.

The real trade would not begin until the discovery of a
land still undreamed of for half a century after Prince Henry's

men explored the West African coast. It was America and
the demand for labor to tame its illimitable territory would
multiply the slave trade from a few hundred to millions, and
would eventually set the states of Africa, Europe, and finally
of the Americas to cutting each others' throats. The trade
would be concentrated on the West African coast from Cape
Verde down, and most especially on what became known as
the Guinea Coast, the thousand mile stretch running nearly
due east in the equatorial latitudes between Cape Palmas
and the Cameroons.

2.

In Prince Henry's time Africa was at once the best and
least known of continents. The history of North Africa was
the history of southern Europe; civilization had begun in
Egypt, whose bas-reliefs often show the negroid profile.
Abyssinia was known to the ancients and in more recent
times had adopted Christianity. Lower on the east coast
there were sophisticated African cities, unknown to Europe
until after the Portuguese finally rounded the Cape of Good
Hope, in 1487, but active in trade with Arabia, India, and
even China. These African cities had all the prerequisites of
Eastern civilization, but since the Orient lacked firearms,
they fell prey to the arms of Portugal.

From the European point of view the undiscovered parts
of Africa in the 1400's were the vast land masses of the interior (though some of its northern territory was known to
Arab traders in the Sahara) and the long coastlines south of
the Canary Islands. The west coast was indeed the only part
of the continent possessed of natural barriers. Even the Sahara was a roadway rather than a barrier for peoples
equipped with camels, horses, and know-how; below it there
were no mountain ranges, no obstructions at all to turn aside
the invader until he approached the equatorial latitudes of
the west coast. This area had a triple defense.

Invaders from the high savannahs of the interior were stopped by the nearly impenetrable rain forests. Arab horsemen could be easily ambushed and cut off when they forced their mounts through the tangle of vines and fallen trees. If they were not, they fell prey to the second line of defense, the tropical insect life. The mosquito brought malaria and yellow fever to the men; the tsetse fly, sleeping sickness to both man and beast.

However, invasion and settlement of the west coast of Africa had been accomplished once upon a time, else the area would not have become so populous as in fact it was. Settlers must have come initially not because anyone fancied the climate, but for the same reason that the Eskimos settled the bleak subarctic—because they were pushed. Once settled, once accommodated to the latitude and given time to develop some resistance to the insect-borne afflictions, the tribes were secure. And when the white men came from the sea, the natives enjoyed the protection of the third line of defense, a coast ringed with heavy surf without a natural harbor between Cape Verde and Luanda in Angola.

The Guinea Coast was unconquerable. True, before the discovery of America, the Portuguese had built the massive fortress Elmina in what is now Ghana, and other fortresses were built as other European nations, even little Brandenberg, entered the trade. But such forts were built only with the consent of the African kings. When in the nineteenth century the Europeans did achieve military conquest, it was possible only because of the devastation wrought on the once flourishing feudal principalities of West Africa by three centuries of a slave trade in which their rulers had connived.

3.

Why did the African rulers voluntarily enter into a trade that was to pervert and nearly destroy their own way of life? With Africans as with Europeans hindsight is easier than foresight. Would the North American settlers have entered the trade if they could have foreseen that its consequences would eventually tear their country apart in the bloodiest of civil wars? Unanswerable, because they could no more foresee such results than the rulers of the wonderful kingdom of Benin could know that their compliance in an immensely profitable trade would destroy the stability of their society and revert their civilization to the savagery that earned for their capital the name of "Benin, City of Blood."

Like the Europeans the African rulers entered the trade for profit. Since their own economy was based on slavery, they had no natural aversion to such commerce. True, African slavery was rather different from what evolved in the Americas and, as will be demonstrated, only certain slaves could legitimately be sold. But there were enough of these to make a beginning, and as the trade became more profitable, the African rules were relaxed.

And how did such trade profit the Africans? Principally because the Europeans possessed much that they did not have and which they learned to covet. If there were advantages in being isolated behind their triple barrier, there were also handicaps. The civilizations that have made the speediest technological progress have usually not been the best protected. Often they have been those which living on a natural crossroads have been conquered and reconquered, learning from each experience.

The West Africans, living apart, had missed many of the inventions of European society. Their tradition was still transmitted orally, and except for some people in the highlands who had learned to write Arabic, they had no alphabet. They had not invented so fundamental a mechanism as the wheel. How should they, when it would have been of no utility in getting them through the rain forests? Only their potters needed such a contrivance; they walked laboriously about their pots instead of turning them.

Nor had even the coastal dwellers learned that cloths could be spread on masts to harness the invisible winds to propel their craft across deep water. It was too hard to reach deep water. This could be done only by the multiple-manned African canoes, which to this day in much of harborless West Africa are the only means of loading and unloading the great ships. And though the West Africans were already well along in the Iron Age, they no more than the East Africans had invented firearms.

When the first Europeans came in the 1440's the Africans were amazed by their white skins, which the Africans had known only as an occasional abnormality, an albino or a leper. They viewed the Europeans with a blend of fascination and repulsion, sometimes apparently confusing their outlandish clothes with anatomical structure.

Once the first shock was over, there was little ambivalence in their attitude toward the white man's technology. They admired, they coveted it: ships that could spread their sails to catch the wind, arms that could magically kill at a distance so much greater than their own iron-tipped spears; gadgets like bells and looking glasses, even scarlet cloths. (African weavers were expert with all shades of blue, but red was beyond them.) Such articles became the substance of their trade with the white men.

When, just before the discovery of America, the Portuguese penetrated the Congo River and met the king they called Don Alfonso, they won a notable convert to their way of life. Alfonso embraced their faith, admitted priests to baptize him and convert his people, sent his son, Prince Henry, to Europe to become a cardinal, and entered into a fraternal correspondence with the King of Portugal.

His cordial letters named the rewards he sought for the slaves he was providing for the Portuguese. He wanted something much better than compliments and gewgaws, something more constructive than firearms. He craved a supply of the medicines that had proved their efficacy against tropical ills; he wanted Portuguese cruzados, he wanted caravels of his own. He did not get them. Ships and cruzados would have enabled the Congolese ruler to trade independently with Europe, and the Portuguese were intent on preserving their monopoly.

The Portuguese did confer one substantial blessing on West Africa; they introduced rice and cassava, both of which quickly became as important to West Africans as potatoes would be to the Irish. The coast was not natively rich in variety of foodstuffs. Its ancient soil, leached by the tremendous seasonal rains, was poor in phosphates. For all the apparent lushness of the rain forests, agriculture was difficult and famine not rare. When the slave trade began in earnest, a trader often found it easier to collect his human cargo than to stock adequate provision for the Atlantic crossing. Without the establishment of the new staples it might have been impossible.

4.

And what was the African way of life before the Europeans transformed it? Or rather, what were the ways of life, for even West Africa was no unity, either ethnologically or politically. The absence of natural barriers in the interior had made Africa a vast melting pot. Hamitic strains had crossed the Sahara from North Africa to mingle with the negroid types. Skin color varied from dark brown with plum plush overtones to coppery tawniness, features from the full lips and spread nostrils of the coastal peoples to the aquiline profile.

Culture ranged from the semi-nomadic life of those on the fringes of the Sahara to the settled agrarian economy of the peoples living near the coast. It was the agricultural know-how of the latter, their skill in clearing and cultivating the land, that made them appear so valuable to the slave traders of North America, where native coastal peoples, still living in a Stone Age culture, gave their best efforts to hunting.

Politically, West Africa possessed great kingdoms like Dahomey, Benin, Mani-Congo, which resembled somewhat
the feudal states of medieval Europe. The luxury of their
courts deeply impressed European visitors, and European
kings dealt with African kings on terms of fraternal equality.
Toward the borders of these kingdoms, royal authority diminished into loosely held fiefs that under pressure dissolved
and merged with each other in cloud-like configurations. In
these outlying areas life seemed like that in Israel in the days
of the patriarchs.

The accounts of the early explorers deal with incidents
on the immediate coast of Africa or with life at the glittering
courts. For a picture of life at the grass roots there is the
story of Mungo Park, a young Scot who came to Africa at the
end of the eighteenth century. It was in this century that
the slave trade reached astronomical proportions, and was
counted in the millions instead of the hundreds. By 1795,
when Park arrived, it had nearly run its course. Competition
for slaves had long since set the coastal kings at each others'
throats, and the demoralizing consequences were so plain
that an occasional ruler attempted to bar his people from
further commerce. Such efforts came too late. Already the
drainage of manpower, the famines brought by frequent
warfare, the decline of ancient tribal moralities had prepared
the unconquerable coast for eventual conquest. It was no
longer possible to stand against the will of the Europeans
and their brothers, the Americans.

Yet young Mungo Park, who penetrated farther inland
than any white man had gone before and lived to tell the
tale, came upon villages where the people still lived in the
primal ways of their ancestors. Park shared those ways, became for the time an adopted child of Africa. When he
journeyed back to the coast, he not only observed the experience of slaves on the road to America, he shared it.

CHAPTER TWO

THE KING'S
STRANGER

DURING the early summer of 1796 the good people of the Niger Valley were bemused by the strange figure cut by a lone youth passing their villages. With his unkempt beard, his lean horse, the fantastic odds and ends of equipment he carried with him, and above all the incomprehensible nature of his errand, he might have been a junior Don Quixote. But unlike the Knight of the Doleful Countenance, he traveled alone.

Who was this, the Bambarra asked each other? He was said to be white, but the term was hardly descriptive. Those parts of him that had not gone leathery with sun had gone yellow with fever. His clothes were vaguely European: a ragged shirt and trousers, a torn waistcoat with a button or two still hanging by a thread, but they were so reduced from their original state that it was hard to be sure. His broken shoes were tied to his feet with thongs. Only his weather-beaten three-cornered hat, in which he carried an untidy sheaf of papers and a little glass object by which he affected to learn his direction, was in anything like its original state.

Most mysterious was his business here. White men who penetrated the interior—they were few and none had come this distance—came for trade. This man denied such a purpose. They had to believe him, for he had nothing to trade with, nothing indeed to live on. The man was a mendicant at the mercy of the Africans. It is a tribute to them that in the long run, where he mercy sought he mercy found.

One lowering evening when the rains threatened, a matron of a village near Sego found him laboriously climbing into a tree near her home. She looked from his emaciated horse, unsaddled for the night, to the starved youth with the fever-bright eyes and asked his business in her tree. Haltingly, in her own tongue, he explained. He had been refused shelter in the huts of the village and was seeking what protection he could from the beasts.

"Follow me," said the matron, and robustly swinging his saddle and bridle to her shoulder, she led the way to her own hut. There she spread a mat for him, lit a lamp, and broiled some fish. And so while the rains came and beat down on his patient horse, the youth lay snug and dry in the hut, watching and listening while his hostess set the women of her compound to their spinning. As they worked, they made up a song calypso style about their guest.

> "The winds roared, the rains fell.
> The poor white man, faint and weary,
> Came and sat under our tree.
> He has no mother to bring him milk,
> No wife to grind his corn.
> Let us pity the white man, no mother has he. . . ."

The spinning and singing went on far into the night, for in these latitudes night is better suited to such labor than day, just as dinner tastes better at midnight than at noon. Spent though he was, the wanderer lay awake to listen, and got his papers out of his hat to make note of the words.

In the morning he took leave of his hostess and made her a present of two of his last four buttons. She accepted with delight; it was not a matter of taking payment for what had been offered out of sheer lovingkindness; she had not invited him in the hope of what was on the coast called a "dash." But buttons were a rare novelty in a land where such robes as were worn flowed free from the shoulders. They were like little jewels, curiously wrought, to be preserved by her children's children.

Soon after, the wanderer was received by the Bambarra king at Sego, who for his part insisted on "dashing" the youth with enough cowrie shells, that served as coin of the realm, to insure that he need not go his way as a beggar. And what, then asked the king, was he seeking here? The Niger, explained Mungo Park, and the king threw up his hands.

"Are there no rivers in his country that he comes so far to see ours?" the king asked.

But he indulged the youth's whim, pressed the cowries upon him, and gave him leave to pursue his crazy journey to the mouth of the river known to the Bambarra as the Jolliba. Such permission was an even more signal act of kindness than the cowries; henceforth, while he remained in the area, he would be known as the king's stranger, a title that deterred the cutthroat.

2.

The youth was Mungo Park, barely turned twenty-five, a surgeon by vocation and an impassioned naturalist by avocation. And he had not entered Africa as a mendicant. The African Association of England had sent him to discover the course of the Niger, of which little had been known since

antiquity, and to ascertain the fate of a prior explorer, Major
Daniel Houghton. Park had begun his expedition with guides
and carriers and sufficient coin and merchandise so that
when he was received by a king he could offer gifts.

His condition by the time he reached the Niger was due
to multiple mischance. Reaching the British outposts on the
Gambia in June 1795 when rains had started, he had fallen
ill of fever. His journey was postponed while he lay in bed,
listening to the pounding of the rain and the sounds of the
African forest at night, "the croaking of the frogs, of which
the numbers were beyond imagination, the shrill cry of the
jackal, and the deep howling of the hyena, a dismal concert
interrupted only by the roar of . . . tremendous thunder."

The delay had brought him one gain. During his conva-
lescence he had time to learn the language of the Mandingoes. This tongue and its dialects he was to meet everywhere
on his travels; without the ability to communicate, and perhaps more important, to understand what was said about
him, it is doubtful that he would have left Africa alive.

But the delay also carried a penalty. When the rains
abated and with them his fever, when he set out in December, the kingdoms of Kaarta and Bambarra were preparing
to take the road against each other in one of the multiple
hostilities unleashed by the pressures of the slave trade. To
avoid being caught on the battleground, he followed advice
and made a wide detour into Ludamar at the edge of the
Sahara. The detour was his undoing.

At first it was a cheerful journey. Once his guides had got
him past the tangle of the rain forests (very wonderfully his
hardy little horse survived the journey), he was in high savannah country, which to his surprise often reminded him
of the rolling uplands of England and Scotland. Even in
their occupations and manners the people were not fundamentally different from the country people at home. Park
found variations in dialect not much more difficult than the

differences between the speech of Yorkshiremen and High-
landers, and by now he was so used to the Mandingoes' color
that he hardly saw it.

But his color was another matter and called for considerable adjustment on the part of the people he met. Though it
was now three centuries since the poor fishermen of Arguin
had bravely paddled their canoes to meet the spirit-ships off
their coast, and the coastal peoples had long since become
sophisticated in the ways of white men, as he went inland,
Park came upon Africans who had never heard that there
existed such creatures as he. Sometimes a lone wayfarer,
coming unexpectedly on the young explorer, resplendent in
his European outfit, every button aglow, and his face still
smooth-shaven and fair, screamed at the sight and fled into
the bush.

In the villages, where people felt security in numbers,
fascination overcame repulsion. They dropped their other
business while they clustered about him to learn what manner of man was this—if it were a man at all. When he paid
his respects to the court at Bondou, which was where he was
advised to make the detour, the ladies of the court couldn't
make enough of him. They pulled off his shoes to count his
toes, peeled off his shirt to see if he were white all over. "His
mother must have dipped him in milk," mused one of them.

His costume attracted as much attention as his skin. In
that day the outfits of a European officer and gentleman
were hardly functional in the tropics; the African, used to
near nakedness in the heat of the day and flowing draperies
in the cool of the evening, sometimes mistook the tight knee-
length breeches, frilled shirt and brass-buttoned waistcoats
for anatomical features. Park's buttons mystified and en-
thralled them, and when he came into Ludamar, he had to
spend the better part of a day buttoning and unbuttoning for
the edification of the Moors of Benowm. No sooner had he
appeased the curiosity of one lot of sightseers when another

came, and he had to begin all over again.

Playing the button game was the least of Park's troubles in Benowm. The Moors of Ludamar were fanatic devotees of Islam, and exhibited nothing of the general African tolerance for infidels and outlanders. With them it was high virtue to destroy or enslave the unbeliever. Park had already learned that Major Houghton, whom he had hoped to find, had been destroyed. Now Park himself, and the one follower who had been willing to venture with him into Ludamar were enslaved. They were seized by the Ali of Benowm, and that the young explorer got away alive was due to the compassion of the Ali's favorite wife.

Park was to pay heartfelt tribute to the women of Africa, and from them he was to receive only kindness. His benefactors were mostly pagan women, but he owed his greatest debt to the Moorish wife of Ali. No less than the woman of Sego, she pitied the bearded youth (he had grown the beard in Benowm when his shaving equipment had been confiscated, and aside from his buttons, it was the one source of prestige he could command there). When her husband's attention was distracted by the first rains, which enabled him to drive his cattle back into the desert, she took the opportunity to restore Park's clothes, his horse, and what equipment she could find. There was little left, none at all of his supplies and money, not even his razor. But she did find his compass and his papers, and thus equipped Park set forth again.

His position was precarious. Nearly everyone he met thereafter knew or at least suspected that he was by rights Ali's prisoner. It took courage on the part of the King of Sego, in fiefage to the Moors, to give aid and comfort to the wanderer, and when Park came through Sego again, he would not risk receiving him at all.

Had Park left with the blessing of Ali, all his property,

and the company of his last attendant (it was a grief to abandon this boy to slavery), his journey would still have been
impracticable. The dry season had passed while he remained
in Benowm, and the onset of the rains, which had enabled
him to escape, would soon make travel entirely impossible.

Yet penniless and alone, already feeling the intermittent
symptoms of a new onslaught of fever, his horse too footsore
and exhausted to bear his weight except on the easiest paths,
the youth pressed crazily on. He had to see the Niger, he had
to ascertain the direction of its flow (since Prince Henry's
time Europeans had somehow supposed it ran west) and he
had to trace it to its mouth. On July 20, 1796, he achieved
the first of these objectives at Sego. He pulled his notes from
his hat to record triumphantly that he was looking at the
Niger "glittering in the morning sun, as broad as the Thames
at Westminster, and flowing slowly *eastward.*" He under-
lined the word that represented his great discovery.

From Sego, fortified by the king's generosity and his permission to proceed, Park went doggedly eastward with the
river, determined to trace it to its outlet. But he didn't get
very much farther. The rain and his fevers were making
travel daily more difficult. What information he could gather
along the way was not encouraging. People could only tell him
that the river ran through countries where strange tongues
and cannibals abounded "to the end of the world." Even so,
Park might have continued had only Negro countries lay
ahead, cannibals or no; what finally stopped him was the
knowledge that Islam lay across his path; he would have no
choice but to pass through the legendary city of Timbuktu.

At the thought of duplicating his experience at Benowm
with probable new refinements of cruelty, even Park's spirit
failed. Far as he was from completing his mission, his only
hope of communicating what he had discovered about the
Niger was to turn back. He made the decision with supreme

reluctance and a sense of apology to the African Association. But make it he did and at last began the painful retracing of his steps.

3.

He faced a journey impossible at this season. The nearest British outpost on the Gambia was 500 miles away. The rains had begun in earnest; the Niger was swelling and flooding its banks, and Park had not enough left of the cowries given him by the King of Sego to pay ferriage for himself and his horse to the western bank. His fever waxed with the rains. At night, after a day spent wading swamps shoulder-high in water, driving his little horse before him, he was often delirious. Ragged and unkempt, when he was lucky enough to travel a bit of the way in company, he felt that the very slaves were ashamed to be seen with him.

He continued on the north bank of the Niger, sometimes swimming its tributaries with his horse's bridle held in his teeth, until the river itself turned south and no longer barred his way. Now he was at the borders of Kaarta and Bambarra, where he could count on a kinder reception than among the Moors. But he must perforce beg his way and this went hard in a country recently reduced to famine by war.

On August 25 Park reached the climax of his miseries. He and his horse were following two shepherds up a precipitous trail between Koona and Sibidooloo when a party of armed Foulahs fell upon them. They stripped the youth of everything but the rags on his back, took even his precious compass, and left him helpless on the hillside.

For the first time Park gave up—better to lie down and die at once than continue his exertions to an end now impossible. But at that moment the impassioned naturalist in him saw a manifestation of Divine Providence. His eye was "irresistibly" caught by the "extraordinary beauty of a small moss in fructification. . . . Though the whole plant was no larger than the top of my finger, I could not contemplate the delicate conformation of its roots, branch and capsula without admiration. Can that Being (thought I) who planted and watered and brought to perfection in this obscure part of the world, a thing which appears of so small importance, look with unconcern upon the situation of creatures formed after His own image? Surely not."

Park picked himself up and somehow managed to catch up with the startled shepherds who supposed that the Foulahs had murdered him. With them he crossed the rocky ridges into Sibidooloo, the frontier town of the kingdom of Manding, where he told his story to the Mansa or headman. "You shall have everything restored to you. I have sworn it!" the Mansa exclaimed when Park had finished, and to an attendant he said: "With the first light of the morning, go over the hills and inform the Dooty of Bamaboo that a poor white man, the King of Bambarra's stranger, has been robbed by the Fooladoo's people."

Such was the Mansa's force of character that Park's property, his horse, his saddlebags, all but his broken compass were sent after him to Wonda, the next village. Because of the famine at Sibidooloo, Park had not wanted to presume too long on the Mansa's generosity, but corn was no less scarce at Wonda. However at Wonda the exhausted youth was taken by paroxysms of fever so violent that for nine days there was no question of his moving on at all. The thought of being a charge on his hosts in hard times made Park feel ashamed, and he used to drag himself out of the hut in the morning to have the worst spasms of illness in a field of corn, out of everybody's sight.

As soon as he was able to travel, on September 8, Park dragged himself away, and by mid-afternoon of September 16 he reached the village of Kamalia, where he was to remain for seven months. Here he found Karfa Taura, the man who would get him back to the Gambia.

4.

The village of Kamalia was spread across a valley floor at the foot of rocky hills, its mud huts with their conical thatched roofs grouped according to the religion of its inhabitants. The center of the town belonged to the Kaffirs, the Negroes who adhered to the old-time religion. The compounds of the Bushreens, or the Negro converts to Islam, were scattered suburban fashion on the outskirts. Kaffirs as well as Bushreens sent some of their children to the school conducted by a devout Bushreen, but one gathers that social prestige belonged to the converts.

Small as the town was, it was of some commercial importance. Gold dust, the most easily transported article of African trade, was washed down to Kamalia from the streams on the hills. The town was also close to the edge of the Jallonka Wilderness, which had to be crossed to reach the trading posts on the Gambia, and so it was a natural stopping place for anyone with anything to sell to the white man. Early as it was in the rainy season, a number of slatees, as the traders were called, had already come in with small lots of slaves. Knowing that Karfa, Kamalia's principal business man, was collecting a coffle to take to the coast, they had stopped to enjoy his hospitality until the furnace blast of the land-wind called the harmattan ushered in the dry season and made travel possible again.

When Park reached Kamalia, he was naturally referred to Karfa. He found him sitting in his baloon, or reception chamber, reading from an Arabic book to some of his guests, the up-country slatees. The traders looked up at Park when he entered the baloon, but they were not impressed. When they heard his story, they refused to believe it, or even that the bearded youth was white.

"It's an Arab," said one slatee.

"He got those European rags by robbery and murder,"

said another.

A proper Arab they would have respected, but an Arab got up in this degrading fashion commanded no consideration. However, the slatees were only guests in Karfa's house, and Karfa pitied the stranger. He devised a test and asked Park to read from his Arabic book. When Park shook his head, Karfa sent for "a little curious book which had been brought in from the west country." Park took this book in his hands and again felt the power of Divine Providence: it was the Book of Common Prayer. He read, and Karfa listened and was convinced. It was not that Karfa, who had never seen a white man before, understood the words. What he did understand was the sense of awe and thanksgiving, the dignity that came over the ravaged youth as again he felt the mercy of the God who had made the moss to fructify.

The reading completed, Karfa addressed himself to the practical problem. He shook his head over the youth's plan to push his way from town to town as fever and rain permitted. Just ahead lay the Jallonka Wilderness, where the distance between towns was often a five days' journey. Passing it was possible only to travelers going in company, carrying their provisions with them, and then only in the dry season, when the eight rapid rivers could be forded. A man traveling alone, unprovisioned, and in the rains, wouldn't have a chance.

"When the rains stop and the grasses are burned, I myself am for the Gambia," said Karfa in effect. "You shall stay and make the journey with me. Can you eat the common victuals of the country?"

Park had long since learned to digest everything deemed edible in these parts, but he could not accept this offer. He had, he explained, no means of paying for his keep. In a country where famine prevailed he could not become a long-term charge upon anyone. He had no choice but to beg his way from town to town, so distributing the burden of his support.

Karfa looked at him long and earnestly, ignoring the mur-
muring of the slatees. Then he thought of the way to restore
his guest's self-respect. Park should have a hut to sleep in,
all he needed to eat, and when the rains abated, safe conduct to the coast. When he got there, he might "make what
return he thought proper." Eagerly Park concluded the bargain. Would the value of "one prime slave" be enough he
asked? When Karfa assented, he went to the hut that had
been swept for him, flung himself down on the mat, and had
out the rest of his fever in peace.

Karfa's other guests, who were also dependent on him to
keep them and their slaves through the rainy season and who
were probably rendered constitutionally suspicious by the
nature of their trade, had little respect for their host's good
sense, and never desisted in their efforts to make him repent
his agreement with Park. Whenever a new trader arrived
from the interior, they cross-examined him to learn what he
knew of Park's mysterious adventures in the Niger Valley.
What they heard, magnified and distorted by rumor, they
carried straight to Karfa and subjected him to such pressures
that Park wondered that he did not yield.

But Karfa was his own man in his own country. Like most
Africans, he trusted and genuinely liked the youth, and he
would not go back on his word. Thanks to him, thanks to the
months in Kamalia, Park acquired nearly as intimate an experience of African life as any African. And when at last he
went on to the coast, he shared a truly African experience,
for he made the journey with a coffle of slaves.

CHAPTER THREE

AFRICAN VILLAGE

THE RAINY season was by
no means a time of uninterrupted deluge, else no one could
have survived it. Though the rain came in sheets, often, especially at the beginning and ending of the season in "tornadoes" attended by violent wind and roaring thunder, it came
in showers only. Days and nights of uninterrupted downpour
were rare, and when they came, were more destructive than
lightning. On a night in the Niger Valley, Park had heard
from his refuge a series of sickening slumps, and in the morning learned that the walls of no fewer than fourteen huts had
caved in during the night. Without an intermission in the
storm the whole village would have collapsed, and there
would have been no shelter at all.

The constant was not so much the rain as the imminence
of it, and though the temperature was lower than during
the dry season, the rains brought a steamy humidity that
infected both physical object and spirit with mildew and
made open fires imperative. Everyone in this season sought
relief by keeping close to a fire. It was a custom that was

already observed in America among the transported Africans. Everywhere, from the West Indies to Virginia, in whatever temperature, the first impulse of African field hands was
to get a fire going at the edge of the field.

For the first five weeks of his stay at Kamalia, Park spent
most of his time lying within the white-washed walls of his
hut, his fever getting worse instead of better. Sometimes
during a sunlit interval between showers he crawled out for
a breath of fresh air; more often he lay all day on his mat,
listening to the drumming of the rain and the drumming of
his feverish heart, waiting for the visits from Karfa's household that interrupted the monotony of his days. Twice daily
a slave came with food; at intervals other slaves came to pour
fresh water into his earthenware jug and carry in firewood.
Once a day he could expect Karfa, who never forgot to come
to ask for his health and assure him that if he kept dry he
would soon be well.

As the rains tapered off, and the ground began to dry,
Park's fever slowly abated. For a long time it left him so
weak that it was all he could do of a bright morning to drag
himself and his mat to the shade of a tamarind tree, where
he could lie enjoying the freshness and watching the corn
shoot up in the fields.

By mid-December, when Karfa left to buy slaves at the
slave market at Kancaba on the Niger, leaving his guest to
the care of the village schoolmaster, Park was enough himself again to resume his study of Africa. He applied himself
to consolidating the notes and the memories he had been
collecting during the past year, and to augmenting them by
intensive observation of the African way of life as he found
it in Kamalia.

2.

Manners were gentle here. Even the presence of two religions side by side, the paganism of the Kaffirs and the Islam

of the Bushreens, and the fact that the latter, an elite minority, unquestionably looked down on the former, did not make for enmity. Park found among Negro Moslems no trace of the fanatic intolerance which made life so difficult for the outlander among the Moors of Benown. The schoolmaster, the most devout Moor of all, who became his best friend after Karfa, was the gentlest man, full of compassionate interest in all humankind, not scornful of differences but eager to learn from them.

Polygamy prevailed among both Bushreens and Kaffirs, at least among men of sufficient means to support multiple households, but here too manners were more gentle than not. Bickering between wives was reduced by the fact that in a well-ordered compound each was queen in her own household; each had her own rights to attention from the husband because of a prescribed order of rotation. To be sure, Park did not enter sufficiently into the intimacies of family life to observe all these details, but it was true that under the best conditions there could be a sisterhood among wives. A good husband would consult his first wife about the choice of a second; she might even devote some of her earnings in the market to contribute towards the new bride's purchase price. And having accepted the newcomer, she might treat her like a younger sister, arranging to exchange marital privileges with her when the lunar cycle interfered with the prescribed rotation.

Polygamy was a unilateral institution. A wife had no corresponding right to a variety of husbands; she could take a new one only if the one she had died, or disappeared for a number of years without communication. Adultery in women was a crime punishable by death or slavery.

Yet the advantages did not lie wholly with the man. As queen in her own household, the wife had first claim on the affections of her children; they clung with warmer affection to their one undisputed mother than to the father whom

they shared with many. Until the children approached the
time of initiation into adult mysteries, she had more to do
with their management than their father, and she continued
to govern her daughters until their own marriages.

Polygamy also insured that no woman would be overbur-
dened with childbearing. While a woman nursed her child—
and children were often nursed through their third year—
it was taboo for her husband to approach her. Park, who was
used to the enormous families common in England at that
time, was surprised to find that few African women bore
more than five or six children. Africans in their turn were to
be amazed and more than a little repelled when long after
Park's time Christian missionaries who reached their towns
had wives who set themselves to producing a baby a year.

The homes Park observed were busy places, giving the lie
to Europeans who dubbed Africans a race of idlers. It took
muscle and persistence for the women and girls to pound the
maize in their pestles into meal for kouskous. And when they
had leisure from preparing food for their households, they
were always at their spinning and weaving. They worked
with cotton thread, coarse but durable, and when the cloth
was woven they turned to dyeing. They pounded fresh indigo leaves in wooden mortars, mixed it with lye and wood
ash in earthen jars, and in the end produced stuffs of lovely
blue, some "with a fine purple gloss." Even the boys turned
their hands to sewing, and the villagers were well clad. The
clothes which the men wore were a kind of loose surplice
over the torso and drawers half way to their knees. The
women wrapped cloth about them as fancy dictated, one
about the waist as a sort of petticoat, the other thrown "neg-
ligently" over their shoulders. The breast was not deemed an
object of shame in these parts.

During the rainy season which Park was able to observe
closely at Kamalia, the older boys were busy in the fields
with their fathers. They worked hard with the short handled

African hoe. Though they worked fewer hours than the farmers of England, and their plots were smaller, the hours were suitable to the climate and the plots were sufficient to raise maize and cotton for their needs. There was no market for a surplus here, and the climate and insects discouraged long-term storage. (Park rated the insects of Africa—he was thinking chiefly of mosquitoes—as a greater menace than its lions or rogue elephants.) If famine was common, it was due not to lack of industry but to seasonal caprice and most of all to the devastation of the wars caused by the merciless pressures of the slave trade.

As the rains ended in December, the men harvested their crops and then went to the bush to hunt or to the rivers to fish, and many of the women laid aside their weaving and climbed the hills to wash gold from the streams. They also had a method of digging it from pits sunk into the ground, but this was done only later in the dry season, and Park did not see them digging for gold.

He spent many days watching the artisans at work. Though gold was collected chiefly for trade with the coast, the women never had enough gold ornaments for their head-dresses. Park watched the goldsmiths smelt the metal and draw it into the fine wires from which the ornaments were fashioned.

He also observed the leatherworkers, but these he had found everywhere in his travels. What was rarer was the African ironworker. (Nearer the coast, where the cheaper European iron was available in quantity, the craft had nearly disappeared.) Park took great interest in visiting the smelting furnace in Kamalia, a circular tower of clay reinforced with withes, with seven openings at the bottom where the fire could be regulated through tubes of baked clay and grass. He himself helped the workmen break the heavy, dull red iron ore, and lay it in the furnace between alternate layers of wood and charcoal. With them he watched the

gradual growth of the fire until it sent flames shooting from
the top of the furnace. The fire burned three days and had to
be let die for as many more before furnace and metal were
cool enough to handle. After that the furnace was dismantled
and the ringing cake-iron removed. He watched the forging
of the iron, hard and brittle but manageable by skilled workmen, into bar iron and spears.

3.

Park's inquiries into the religious beliefs of the Kaffirs
yielded more superficial information. Possibly his attitude
was at fault. His scientific detachment did not extend to the
study of religions different from his own; as a good church-
man he was prone in the privacy of his journal to dismiss the
religious practices he saw as "superstition." Although he was
too well bred to make such comments openly, and indeed
honored harmless customs, like contributing a cloth of his
own to hang on the mumbo jumbo tree on whose branches
every passerby was expected to hang such an offering, his
feelings may have been subtly communicated to the Kaffirs.

He may also have been at a disadvantage because he was
a guest of a Moslem, and it is possible that in Kamalia the
prestige of the Moslems had caused a decline in primitive
religious practice. Though the majority remained Kaffir, it
was the Moslems who worshipped publicly—in fair weather
in an open air mosque, enclosed by tree trunks, with a small
platform facing east where the marabout stood to summon
the faithful to prayer.

Park saw an occasional funeral and some of the more
public aspects of the initiation rites, but the only Kaffir ceremony that struck him as having true religious content was
performed on the appearance of the new moon, which the
Kaffirs believed had been newly created. With hands held
before their faces, they whispered a prayer of thanksgiving
to God for preserving them during the life of the old moon

and a plea for protection through the life of the new one. Then they spit on their hands and rubbed them over their faces.

What impressed Park was that the prayer acknowledged the existence of God, who otherwise received little attention from the Kaffirs. They thought him "a being so remote and of so exalted a nature that it [was] idle to suppose the feeble supplications of wretched mortals [could] reverse the decrees and change the purpose of unerring wisdom." They were more concerned with minor deities, unspecified by Park, whose intercession in human affairs could be induced by offerings of a white fowl, a snake's head, fruit.

The Kaffirs vaguely acknowledged a belief in life after death but would not describe it to him. "No one knows anything about it," they would say in an embarrassed attempt to close the discussion. If they spoke truly, but they probably did not, they had a most atypical African religion. The concept of a remote God and the more approachable tutelary deity was common enough in Africa, but the Kaffirs' vagueness about the world of the dead was unprecedented. In Dahomey, a short journey to the southeast, the way to the kingdom of the dead had been charted as explicitly as the Mandingoes had charted the way through the Jallonka Wilderness: so many rivers to cross, so much ferriage to be paid (the dead were provided with the fares) and at last a hill to climb. And almost universally among the true Negroes, the presence of the dead, of ancestors immediate and remote, was felt as a natural part of daily life. But this the Kaffirs of Kamalia were not discussing with a man of outlandish breed whose protector was a Bushreen.

For his part Park pitied their ignorance and wished that missionary work among them had not been left to the Moslems. Unlike the Portuguese, the English had so far done nothing to impart their own religion to Africans, and the latter had little reason to suppose that the white man had any. They "look on us, I fear, as little better than a race of formidable but ignorant heathen."

4.

Park had more fruitful discussions with the old school-master Fantooma. Gentle, devout without bigotry, the old man was a born scholar and, like Chaucer's Clerk of Oxenford, "of bookes tooke he moste cure and heed." His library, much of it painstakingly copied in his own hand, included not only the Koran and its commentaries, but Arabic versions of the Pentateuch, the Psalms of David, and the Book of Isaiah. Park was not surprised. Though he had learned little of Kaffir religions, he had discovered long before reaching Kamalia that familiarity with the Old Testament was not uncommon in this part of Africa. Unlettered Mandingoes had entertained him by recounting as part of their own lore the stories of Joseph and his brethren, of Moses, of David and Solomon, and they were astonished to find that the white men knew them too. Did the prevalence of such lore merely demonstrate the catholic interests of the true Moslem scholar, or had Park happened upon an area where Jewish communities may have taken refuge after the Dispersal? He had never heard of such communities and did not raise the question. He was too interested in studying Fantooma's methods as a schoolmaster.

In the old man's schools there were seventeen "slaves," all boys, and two girls, one a daughter of Karfa. The girls got their lessons by day; the boys spent the daylight hours fetching wood and cultivating Fantooma's fields, and only before dawn and after sundown did they gather about a large fire to receive instruction. They were working their way, hence the term "slave." In a country where hired free labor was unknown, there was no other term.

The children learned to write by copying Arabic letters on papers, and to read by shouting in chorus at the top of their lungs passages from the Koran. Most were children of Kaffirs, who had sent them to Fantooma not from any fervor for Islam, but because in these parts there was no other way of becoming literate. Looking at the earnest, bright-eyed youths, shouting their exercises in the Koran, Park thought that they would have as gladly learned the catechism of the Church of England had such instruction been available.

The school had no set terms, for this was a culture that took no account of time in white man's sense, except as it concerned fast and feast days. A scholar graduated when he was ready, when he had read the Koran through and had performed an assigned number of public prayers. Then Fantooma prepared a feast and invited the Bushreens to enjoy it and to examine his scholars. Park attended three such functions and noted that the questions were searching and the replies intelligent. When the oral examination ended, the scholar read aloud the final page of the Koran, pressed it to his forehead and said Amen. At that all the Bushreens arose, shook him by the hand, and invested him with their title.

There remained one more formality. The parents had to redeem their children from school by bringing Fantooma the equivalent of the value of a slave. On the rare occasions when they lacked means to do so, the boy remained in the status of domestic slave until he earned enough to buy himself free.

Like Park, Fantooma was waiting for the return of Karfa and the departure of the coffle, which he would join until it reached his own village. When at last the coffle set out, Fantooma took with him eight undergraduates, eight young scholar-slaves.

CHAPTER FOUR

COFFLE TO
THE COAST

BY APRIL 1797, Park privately despaired of seeing the Gambia again. Travel had been possible since February; the season was favorable, and the coffle was ready. Karfa had long since returned from Kancaba with fourteen slaves. One girl would not continue the journey; Karfa had found in her too much grace to be wasted on the white men and had raised her to the rank of fourth wife. That being settled, there seemed no further cause to tarry, but still they tarried. Park feared that the rains would be on them again before anyone could be induced to move.

The rains had begun to subside in November, their ending like their beginning marked with "tornadoes." Later the wind, which during the rains had blown steadily from the southwest, shifted to the northeast and the harmattan came in from the Sahara like a blast from the furnace. It parched the country in days and brought heat and a dust-laden haze that chapped the lips and inflamed the eyes. It also brought or was capable of bringing meningitis, but Park was fortunate enough not to know that. After the prolonged steam bath of the rains, the wind was a bracer to him. The last traces of his fever went with the moisture and the mildew. Park was ready for adventure.

When the harmattan had dried the grasses, the Mandingoes set them on fire, and Park saw "a scene of terrific grandeur. In the middle of the night I could see the plains and mountains, as far as my eye could reach, variegated with lines of fire; and the light reflected on the sky made the heavens appear in a blaze." By day he saw pillars of smoke, and birds of prey hovering to pounce on snakes and lizards trying to escape the flames. Park does not say what happened to the other beasts. Perhaps the communities of lions, elephants, and antelopes had adjusted their culture to the burnings, as American deer seem to adjust to the hunting season.

Such fires are still characteristic at this season in the West African bush. They can be observed by night from the air, not extending as Park saw them "from horizon to horizon," but in rings and horseshoes. Agricultural experts deplore them as destructive; Africans defend them as necessary to remove the fire hazard of tall grasses close to the thatched roofs of their villages and to speed the growth of new grass. Park himself thought the fires were beneficial: the soil still held enough rain to protect the roots, and as the fires receded the new grasses and foliage sprang up in miraculous abundance in place of the rank tangle of the old.

In February he was gladdened by seeing preparations for departure. But the preparations were prolonged interminably. Some members of the coffle had yet to arrange their supplies of dry provision; others went off to say good-bye to relatives or to collect debts. Finally, late in the month, when the slatees had begun calculating the lucky day for travel, they realized that the fast of Ramadan was upon them, so the trip was postponed "until the fast moon was over."

Park steadied his nerves by fasting with them, not for the whole month, but for three days, just long enough to save his host from the reproach of entertaining a Kaffir. He attended the morning readings and prayers conducted by the schoolmaster at Karfa's house, watched the Bushreen wives, clad all in white, prostrate themselves at their evening devotions at the Misura. He was impressed with the solemn humility with which these Negroes accepted Islam as against "the savage intolerance and brutal bigotry which at this period characterized the Moors."

2.

The long wait for their departure for the coast, tedious though it was, gave Park time to consolidate his impressions of African slavery. Its most striking characteristic was its two categories, foreign and domestic. Only foreign slaves were normally used in the trade. A domestic slave could be sold only for his own misconduct or his master's need, and then only after a palaver of the village elders to judge the merits of the case. This distinction prevailed in Africa; in some parts the pressure of the trade was said to be extinguishing the rights of the domestic slave, but this Park did not observe among the Mandingoes.

The foreign slaves had been taken by capture or purchase from another nation, or at least another village. Some were criminals, for murder, adultery, kidnapping, and witchcraft were so punished.

Some domestic slaves were descendants of prisoners of war. Most had entered servitude as the result of debt or need. A man might pledge his body for a debt, and if he could not pay, his body was forfeit. The custom bore some resemblance to the English debtors' prisons of Park's day. The difference was that the English condition was not hereditary, except as circumstances inflicted the same fate on the debtors' children, and that the African debtor by no means languished in idleness.

The commonest cause of domestic slavery was famine, which forced men to sell their birthright of freedom for a mess of pottage. Since the scorched earth policy attending the wars was the principal cause of famine, war brought domestic no less than foreign slavery. Park had seen a woman in Wonda who had sold her five-year-old son to get a ration of corn for the rest of her family. Whenever she came to draw her ration, she fondled the child and talked with him. Mother and son were cheerful on these reunions, and with reason. Though the child and his descendants were committed to slavery (and if the Mandingo belief resembled that of Dahomey, a slave's very soul would continue to serve his master in the next world), his estate was not unhappy. He had been given a kind master who would not let him go hungry and would not be allowed to sell him except in case of supreme emergency. If the master's heirs were less kind, if the slave were abused, he could appeal for protection to the village elders.

In a land without a tradition of free labor, without even a vocabulary to identify it, the system of domestic slavery seemed to Park more humane than not. Often master and slave worked together in the fields without visible distinction. To be sure, in time of war, when the master carried a spear or musket, the slave carried the supplies and was therefore more apt to fall into foreign captivity than his master. But in the confusion of battle the slave sometimes got hold of a weapon, and if he distinguished himself, especially if he took two captives, he might win his freedom. (The usual price for redeeming a slave was on a two-to-one basis.) Women slaves who found favor in the eyes of their lords might become acknowledged wives, as had happened to the comely girl Karfa had brought home from Kancaba. Even if they became only concubines, in subservience to the wives, their children were free.

In Kamalia it seemed to Park that domestic slaves enjoyed
the same fare as their masters, amused themselves in the
same ways, and were not displeased with their lot. He dis-
mayed his friends, many of whom were abolitionists, by re-
marking in the book he wrote as soon as he got back to Scotland that Africans in general were not yet ready for freedom.
His statement was cryptic at best, but it is improbable that
when he made it his mind was on the lot of the "foreign"
slaves.

In Kamalia, Park saw a great deal of the foreign slaves
awaiting transportation to the coast. The tamarind tree where
he dragged himself during intermissions of his fever was the
one they sat under during the day. All these slaves were
weighed down with heavy leg irons, and being allowed no
exercise beyond that of hauling themselves in and out of their
huts, they were almost losing the use of their limbs.

Aside from the irons, which were carefully examined every
evening before the slaves were put back in their huts under
the guard of Karfa's domestic slaves, Park saw no evidence of
cruel treatment. The foreign slaves were adequately fed and
allowed to spend their days under the tamarind playing
games of hazard and singing. Two of them were sullen and
would not talk, at least to Park; one somehow got hold of a
knife and escaped; the rest endured their lot with apparent
resignation.

Talking with them, Park found that the majority had been
slaves since birth, and they were preferred by the slatees as
being inured to the fatigues of labor since childhood and the
less likely to give trouble. But others were casualties of the
late war between Bambarra and Kaarta. One man had befriended Park during his destitute wanderings in the Niger
Valley by giving him milk. "But then I had no irons on my
legs," the slave said sadly.

Sometimes it was the slaves who did the questioning. They
thought of the whites as a sort of sea creature, and assumed

that they had no use for slaves except as meat. Park took pains to describe the plantations in the Americas, to assure them that they would be well fed and cared for, given the same work that they were used to. They looked at him with sad incredulity.

"Have you really got such ground as this," asked one of them, putting his hand to it, "to set your feet on?"

Park could not convince them. The slaves sat under their tree, reluctant even to loose the chains that chafed them, for they knew that such a loosing would be the signal for them to march to meet the white-skinned cannibals from the sea.

3.

On April 19 the coffle set out at last. The day had been selected by the slatees after diligent moon-watching and palavers over lucky days. The fast of Ramadan could not be declared at an end until the new moon was sighted, and the night of its scheduled appearance was overcast. When the moon came out, the Bushreens made a joyful noise unto the Lord; they clapped hands, beat drums, fired muskets. And now, since this was the luckiest of moons, Karfa gave orders for the final preparations.

When the expedition marched, the entire town marched with it. Women wept and clung to departing husbands; friends and relatives clasped hands. On a slight rise, half a mile from town. Karfa commanded a halt. Members of the coffle were ordered to sit in one place, their faces to the west; the villagers in another, with their faces to the east, to Kamalia. Between them old Fantooma and two slatees stood to invoke the blessing of Allah on traveler and stay-at-home.

Ahead of the travelers lay the tangle of rain forest, crocodile infested rivers, prides of lions, herds of elephants, swarms of insects more deadly than any beast, and human enemies. Nor could the people remaining in Kamalia count on peace. Wars and rumors of wars were constant in the century of the great trade and there were always bands of raiders about.

So the schoolmaster and his companions prayed long and earnestly, and when that was done, performed a rite that was perhaps older than Islam. Three times they circled the coffle, stabbing at the ground with their spears. Then abruptly they were off. Without another word of leave taking, without a backward glance, every member sprang to his feet and began the march.

The first day's march was not long; they got only to Bala, the second village beyond Kamalia. The slaves who were destined for trade and released from the leg irons they had worn for weeks or years, had a difficult time getting that far. Until the first day of the march they had hardly had occasion to stand upright; now, roped together in lots of four, each with a burden on his head, they could barely walk, and their attempt to obey the command of quickstep brought on muscular spasms. A scant mile beyond Kamalia two were in such pain that they had to be left. The ropes were loosed to detach them from their yokes, and domestic slaves were assigned to keep them under guard and bring them up to the party as soon as possible.

Other slatees and their slaves awaited the coffle in each of the two towns beyond Kamalia. It was only on the afternoon of April 20, when the party left Bala, that the coffle was complete. The party numbered seventy-eight, thirty-five of whom were human merchandise intended for export. The rest were freemen, their wives, and their domestic slaves, the latter including the eight pupils of Fantooma. All but the slaves carried spears, and everyone went on foot. Park had long since sent his faithful little horse back to Wonda as a gift to his benefactor there, and though Karfa had a number of asses, they were broken in to carry packs, not riders.

Park does not say what merchandise was being transported along with the slaves. They certainly had gold dust, perhaps some ivory, and Karfa had strings of beads with which he sometimes purchased food. They also had "dry provision," but this was designated for an emergency, like the five-day march through the uninhabited center of the wilderness, rather than for daily fare. It would probably have been impractical to carry enough food for so many on a journey of 500 miles. The plan was to buy provision on the way, or to have the six jillakeas, or singing men, sing for their supper. Some of the latter were also traders with slaves of their own for sale, but they rendered service to the party at large. It was they who won admission to walled towns by hymning the virtues of the inhabitants before the gates; en route they beguiled the tedium of the way with songs and jokes.

The journey ahead was long and hard, and it was not the will of Allah that everyone should survive its dangers. Yet when the march went smoothly, it seems likely that even the slaves enjoyed it. To rediscover the mastery of their limbs, as most of them did after the first day or so, was an almost sensuous pleasure. The ropes on their necks were light after the weight of the chains on their legs, and though they carried the chains with them, the irons were ordinarily used only at night or for special cause. Their fate, dreadful or not, still lay so many miles, so many days ahead of them that it could be disregarded. Some of them, grateful for Park's reassurances whether they believed him or not, took him under their care. Park was touched by their solicitude in getting water for him during the stops, or in breaking branches and gathering leaves to make him a couch.

On the morning of April 21 they left the last outpost of Manding, and at the border of the country of the Jallonkadoo stopped for another solemnity. Fantooma offered a prayer "that God and the holy prophet might preserve us from robbers and all bad people, that our provision might never fail us nor our limbs be fatigued."

And now, since they were no longer among their own people, the party was disciplined into strict protocol when-

ever it approached a town, and formed a procession ranged
in prescribed order. At the head walked the singing men, behind them came the free men, next the slaves in groups of
four, each attended by an armed guard, then the domestic
slaves, and last the free women.

In this order they came to Kinyatakoora and waited in their
ranks while the singing men stood at the gates, praising the
town's reputation for hospitality, recounting proofs of their
long friendship with the Mandingoes. Kinyatakoora was a
town untouched by famine, able to perform the rites of holy
hospitality, and delighted with the entertainment offered by
so notable a party. The gates were thrown open, and the
coffle invited to take places about the Bentang, a platform
that served as a kind of open-air town hall. Children ran
shouting into the compounds to tell their mothers, and the
whole town gathered to enjoy a major social event.

Now began the longest task of the singing men: the chanting of a Homeric narrative about their journey. Two singers
began by reciting events of that day's march and worked
backwards, including the most trivial detail, until they had
got to the departure from Kamalia. That completed their
share of the entertainment; it was time for the town to offer
theirs. The master of the town began by "dashing" each
singer with a small present. Then one by one the towns-
people came forward to invite the members of the coffle,
slave and free, to share their huts for the night and their provisions.

Thus comfortably, even gaily, did matters go on the line
of march when people were friendly and conditions pleasant.
But not everyone was friendly and conditions could be very
unpleasant.

Park, who had nearly lost his life among Foulah raiders
before he came to Kamalia, now heard of them again. They
had been raiding the Jallonkadoo, and close to the hospitable
town of Kinyatakoora the coffle found the charred remains

of two small towns laid waste by the raiders, and found the people of another village in the act of fleeing to a fortified situation among the rocks of a steep hill. When the travelers found the prints of many hooves in the soft sands of a river, they abandoned the easy route and broke up into small parties. So that their footprints would not be seen by any Foulahs, they struggled through tall grass and underbrush. In another Jallonkadoo town they were admitted to the huts grudgingly and denied food on the excuse of famine. Shelter was necessary, however, for the rains were coming on, and Park's fear that they had delayed the journey too long was justified. Even so, on one threatening night they avoided a town altogether because of its reputation for thievery and laboriously constructed their own temporary huts.

People got left behind and had to be searched for and waited for. Once it was a free woman whom everyone supposed to have been devoured by a lion until she was found sleeping comfortably by a stream. Once it was a quartet of slaves and their guard. The slaves had enforced the delay in the hope of escaping, but they had not been able to snatch the guard's spear. By threatening to stab them one by one, the guard succeeded in marching them up to the rest of the party.

At one famine-stricken town it was the coffle who regaled the villagers with a feast of kouskous, for which they were "rewarded" by the kidnapping of one of the Fantooma's boys from under the Bentang tree, where he had fallen asleep. No one heard the lad's screams, and only his wits saved him: he pointed out to his captor that Fantooma's village was only three days distant and would certainly avenge the kidnapping. Finally the boy returned to camp, unharmed but naked. The captor had stripped him.

The slaves suffered the most serious mishaps, however. Two of them, a woman and a girl, fell so ill that at Kinyata-koora their master had no choice but to lead them home

again. The cause of their ailment was discovered when they
vomited clay. "Dirt eating" was common in Africa, and already in the Americas it was bedeviling masters, some of
whom used a muzzle to discourage the practice. Done in
moderation it was apparently an indulgence like chewing
gum or tobacco, and had possibly developed as a means of
allaying hunger in times of famine. Consumed in quantity,
clay was supposed to be a means of suicide, and that was the
probable objective of the two slaves. They had produced an
illness serious enough to defeat their master's purpose of selling them to the American traders.

A miserable fate befell another slave girl, Nealee. She was
the property of Karfa, probably one of the lot he had bought
at Kancaba, where he had found his fourth wife. Poor Nealee
lacked the charm for so happy a solution to slavery. What
her personal tragedy was, beyond the obvious, Park had no
idea, for she was a sullen girl who confided in no one. From
the first day she had given trouble, often refusing to eat, and
on the fifth, when the coffle struck across wild and rocky
country that bruised the feet, she complained of unbearable
pains in her legs. It became so difficult for her to move that
Karfa gave her load to another slave, which did not contribute to her popularity.

At noon that day, while the coffle rested by a small stream,
someone discovered a hive of bees in a hollow tree and went
after the honey. The bees counterattacked, in incredible numbers and with such fury that the party was stampeded. Park,
who had been watching the tree, was the first to see the danger and run; he alone escaped unharmed. The rest of the
coffle fled too late, dropping their bundles in their panic as
they tried to protect their faces. Nothing could induce the
slaves to return for their burdens until a fire had been set
well to the east of the hive; only when it had gained headway
in the wind would they pick their way through the smoke
and retrieve their bundles.

They found more than their provisions: they found tragic Nealee, and at first they hardly knew her. Caught in the center of the swarm of bees and unable to run with the rest, her attempt to take refuge in the shallow stream had been useless. Her whole body was swollen with the stings, and such was her agony that she pleaded to be let die where she lay.

The slatees did what they could. They washed her, picked out the stings, rubbed her wounds with bruised leaves; but they had to lash her to force her to move. For four hours Nealee managed to keep up, moaning pitifully, and then made an attempt to escape, only to collapse in the grass. This time she was indifferent to the lash. Karfa ordered her placed on an ass, but when the beast refused to carry her, Karfa had the slaves make a litter of bamboos tied together with bark and carry her so.

The day was hot. The party was traveling on short rations, and everyone's wounds burned and stung. When they stopped for the night, the slaves gave signs of mutiny by snapping their fingers, which, according to Park, was an ominous sign among Negroes. Though the party was deep in the wilderness, where fugitives would have small chance of survival, Karfa had the slaves put in chains for the night.

The next day was worse. Nealee, stiff with pain, could neither stand nor walk. She was lifted like a corpse to the back of an ass, her hands fastened together under his neck, her feet tied under his belly. But the beast would have none of a human burden. He bucked and threw her, trussed up as she was, and Nealee made no effort to save herself.

From the members of the coffle, slave and free, a murmur grew to a shout. "Kang-tegi! Kang-tegi!" This meant, "Cut her throat." Park walked on ahead, too sick to watch.

But Nealee's throat was not cut. Neither Fantooma nor Karfa would permit it; instead they left her to Allah. The miserable woman was given what she asked for, placed in the bush off the path and left to die. Given the prevalence of beasts (they met elephants later that day), it might have been kinder to cut her throat.

No one shouted now against Nealee. Even the singing men found no subject for song as they plodded on, unable to forget the girl's fate or that anyone else might share it. Fantooma, deeply saddened, fasted for twenty-four hours, and Park, finding that keeping up with the coffle took every last ounce of his strength, threw away his spear. It was useless against the real perils of Africa.

4.

On April 25 the coffle crossed the Bafing River on a floating bridge ingeniously constructed of bamboos lashed across two tall trees, which were placed so that while each tree was firmly rooted in the banks of the river, the tops of the trees floated midstream. The bridge had to be rebuilt after each flood, and the inhabitants of Manna, who had engineered it, collected a toll.

On May 2 Fantooma sent a runner ahead to his native Malacotta to order a feast prepared. The messenger returned to the party with Fantooma's elder brother, who had not seen him for nine years. From the stream where Park was swimming, he watched a touching reunion: Fantooma and his brother fell on each other's necks and embraced speechlessly, drew back to wipe their eyes and embraced again. It was moments before Fantooma regained his poise.

"This is the man who has been my father in Manding," he said introducing Karfa to his brother. "I would have pointed him out before, but my heart was too full."

For three days the coffle enjoyed the hospitality of Malacotta, and on each day Fantooma contributed a bullock to the feast. During this stop Park had time to examine the local industries: he admired the way the huts were constructed of wickerwork of split cane plastered with mud, the local method of making good soap by adding a lye of wood ashes to boiled ground nuts, their superior craft in smelting and fashioning iron, which they traded with Bondou for salt.

In Malacotta the singing men added to their repertoire a remarkable new tale: the unprecedented outcome of a recent war between King Almami Abdulkader of Foota Torra and King Damel of the Jaloffs, whose domains lay between the Gambia and Senegal Rivers. King Almami had begun it by offering the Jaloff ruler the choice of embracing Islam or having his throat cut. Objecting to both alternatives, Damel had retreated from village to village, carrying out a scorched earth policy as he went, so that Almami found all wells stopped up and provisions destroyed. Finally, when the Foulah had been worn out by such tactics, Damel led a crushing counterattack and captured the king.

Custom called for Damel to put his foot on the neck of the aggressor and his spear through his heart. Instead he made a speech: "My spear is red with the blood of your subjects dead in battle, and I could now give it a deeper stain by dipping it into your own," said Damel. "But this would not build up my towns, nor bring to life the thousands who fell in the woods. I will not therefore kill you in cold blood, but I will retain you as my slave until I perceive that your presence will no longer be dangerous to your neighbors."

After three months, during which the king humbly performed his duties as slave, Damel actually returned him to the chastened people of Foota Torra. This was the strangest chapter in African military history that Park had ever heard, but after he had heard it from many sources, including people from Foota Torra, he believed it.

After the coffle left Malacotta and Fantooma, happily reunited with his family, there were other reunions. At Baniserile the intended bride of one of the slatees knelt before him holding a calabash of water. When he had washed his hands in it, the girl lovingly drank the water. This act of devotion made the traveler decide to leave the party and marry his bride. But there was also a mercenary consideration: the slatee had learned that slaves were not at the moment getting a good price on the Gambia, and while he tarried with his love, conditions were bound to improve.

The coffle was drawing near to the coast. In Medina they lodged with a Mandingo merchant who affected European ways, even to the construction of his house and the serving of food in pewter dishes. During the two-day march through the thick woods of the Tenda Wilderness they met a coffle returning from the Gambia with European hats on their heads, scarlet cloths over their shoulders, and muskets in their hands. But their news was discouraging: no ship had arrived for months, and there was little demand for slaves. A group of Serawoolli traders, who had attached themselves to Karfa's party a few days earlier, left the coffle and struck off to the north with their slaves.

For a long time the land had been sloping downward to the coast. Because the heat was increasing and the water supply diminishing, Karfa decided to risk traveling by night. Doing so was hazardous, not only because wild beasts were most active then, but because the slaves, who could not be marched any distance in chains, might more easily escape in the darkness. But ordering his party to close ranks, Karfa set out one evening near midnight.

The next noon they stopped at the walled town of Tambacunda and did not go on for four days. A delicate crisis had arisen: the slatee Modi Lemina had left there a wife and two children; in fact, he had left them there for eight years, without giving any account of himself in the meantime. Now when he presented himself, eager to reward wifely fidelity, he found that the woman had a new husband and two more children.

It took a four-day palaver to settle the matter. Polygamy is for husbands, not wives. Nevertheless, an abandoned wife has her rights; after three years she may consider herself a widow and act as one. The elders of the town came to a judgment: the woman should choose which husband she would keep. The woman said she needed time to think it over, and while she did so, Karfa's party moved on.

Even now, so close to the Gambia that they began crossing its branches, their troubles were not over. They had to keep a wary lookout for Foulah raiders who haunted this area to drive off herds of cattle and enslave the herdsmen. The season was wearing on towards June, and as Park had anticipated, the first rains were catching them on the road. They often walked in a downpour, each man carrying what Park called "the Negro umbrella," the great leaf of the ciboa palm.

Just short of their entrance to what the singing men hymned "the land of the setting sun," one of the singers exchanged a slave who had gone lame for a young girl from the little villages called collectively Tenda. It was not considered necessary to consult the girl on the matter. She had come out for the fun of watching the coffle depart when she was seized and roped and a load was placed on her head. The girl's terror, the grief with which she said good-bye to her companions afflicted Park almost as much as had the fate of poor Nealee.

But that very afternoon Park forgot everything in his joy at finding himself on the banks of the Gambia. For eighteen months "I had not beheld the face of a Christian, nor once heard the delightful sound of my native language." He was approaching friends who would receive him "as one risen from the dead."

For the time being this was the journey's end for most of the slaves. Karfa took Park's advice to settle his group on a plot at Jindey, where they could break the soil and raise their own provisions while awaiting the white man's ships. Not without emotion Park took leave of the slaves, who had been as concerned for his comfort as Karfa himself, and again he assured them that the white men were not cannibals, that a

happy life awaited them in the world beyond the seas.
Though they did not believe him, they were fond of him.
White man and slaves blessed each other in parting, each
after his own fashion.

Park set out to find his friends, and Karfa went with him.
It was a point of honor with Karfa to restore his guest in
person to the company of his own kind.

5.

And now every day the good Bushreen of Kamalia, who
had never visited the coast before, saw a new constellation
of wonders. He stopped with Park at the home of one Camilla, who, though a Negro, had lived among white traders
for years, spoke their language and lived in European style.
While Park was convincing Camilla that he was really he—
he had changed unrecognizably in the two years since she
had last seen him, and besides word had come that he had
been killed by the Moors of Ludamar—Karfa was dividing
his attention between the remarkable sound of English palaver and the strange sights of the household. When he had
Park's ear again, he had a hundred questions about the objects he saw, the chairs with their legs, the bed with its cur-
tains.

At Pisana, where they went on June 10 on the invitation of
a white man, Karfa saw something that sent him into amazed
meditation for the rest of the day, a schooner riding at anchor
in the river. Even with Park beside him to explain masts, rig-
ging, and sails, Karfa was as incredulous as the fishermen who
first met Prince Henry the Navigator and couldn't believe
that an invisible element like air could be harnessed to move
a boat. More plausible was Park's explanation of the hull, and
Karfa admired the skill with which the planks had been fastened and the seams sealed up against the water.

Park himself became the subject for wonder when his old
friend Dr. John Laidley appeared, bringing Park's clothes

and shaving equipment. Karfa watched fascinated as Park put on European clothes, complete with buttons, but was desolated when Park shaved off his beard.

"I found a man," said Karfa. "I leave a boy."

It was a grateful boy. Before leaving Kamalia, Park had written down an order to the African Association to deliver Karfa the price of one slave, even if he, Park, failed to reach the coast alive. Now he doubled the amount and added a "handsome present" for the old schoolmaster, Fantooma, all to be delivered in goods whenever Karfa found it convenient to send for them.

"My journey has indeed been prosperous," said Karfa solemnly, and looking about him at the manifold ingenuities of white man's civilization, his African pride was humbled. "Fata fing, inta fing," he said. "Black men are nothing."

For the first time, like the King at Sego he wondered why Park had come. What, he seriously and repeatedly asked, had induced Park, who was no trader, to come "to so miserable a country as Africa?" What was there here to hold the attention of one who every day in the year could observe wonders at home?

Park and Karfa parted on June 14, when Karfa returned to look after his party in Jindey. They parted affectionately, but without ceremony, for Park had little prospect of leaving the Gambia before the end of the year and expected to see his friend again. Indeed, he was to do so, but not for many years. On the very next day the *Charleston*, an American vessel, entered the river, immediately made up its cargo of slaves and took on Park as passenger, though at Goree he was to become ship's surgeon.

So it was given Park to complete the journey of the coffle, though not the original coffle he had set out with, for the factories on the Gambia were glutted with slaves; Karfa still had to wait his turn at other ships. But two on the *Charleston* had seen him in his travels, and many others had heard of him. They were blessed in Park's being aboard; he was almost like one of their own, and he could speak to them in their own tongue.

Park was shocked by the conditions on board an American slaver. Master and crew were not deliberately cruel, but because the ship was undermanned, the slaves were confined and shackled with a severity he had never seen on British ships. The ship was overcrowded with its cargo of 130 slaves, and sickness set in at once. Three were dead before they left the Gambia; eight more died at Goree, and in spite of Park's best efforts, eleven died on the voyage, and many of the rest were barely alive when they made their landfall. This was Antigua, a leak in the vessel having forced the master to take the shorter course. Park was lucky enough to board a packet almost at once and to reach England in time for Christmas, 1797.

He had not seen the last of Africa. They say there is something about the place that draws the traveler back. At home Park organized his notes and wrote a book, which being the first of its kind made him famous. The Duchess of Devonshire contributed to it by rendering the song of the women of Sego into English meter and having the words set to music. Park married happily, had children, and set up practice in Scotland as a country doctor. But like Tennyson's Ulysses he could not rest from travel, and in 1805 he accepted an invitation to lead another expedition to Africa.

This call came not from the private gentlemen of the African Association but from the British government. England's interest in Africa had progressed from the slave trade, which it would suppress after 1807, to colonialism. The English trading posts on the Gambia, in Sierra Leone, the Gold Coast were already forming the nucleus of colonies. Eventually the British would control the vast territory of Nigeria, named for the great river on which it now asked Park to pursue his investigations.

For the Niger was still a mystery. Park had demonstrated that its course was to the east and that it was one of the great rivers of Africa, second in importance only to the Nile and the Congo. But no one knew where it emptied, how far it was navigable, or what prospects of commerce lay along its banks. And Park, now convinced that the Niger joined the Congo, set forth on a second voyage of discovery.

He reached the Gambia late in April 1805, and though the rainy season had begun and none knew better than he the unwisdom of travel during the rains, he set his expedition on the road at once. Why? Was he overawed by his responsibility as representative of the British government, which had invested heavily in this undertaking? Did he suppose that British soldiers, of whom he had been assigned a company of thirty-five volunteers were immune to African ills? Whatever his reasoning, fever struck down his men at once; some had to be left behind, some died, one went mad. When he reached the Niger in November only half a dozen were left. The diminished party started downstream on a raft, and the Africans who had been kind to the penniless youth traveling unarmed and alone, took every opportunity to harry the man who had returned in the company of soldiers with muskets.

"If I do not succeed in reaching my goal, I will go to meet my death on the Niger," Park had written in a message sent back with the guide Isako. And that was the last word he ever sent; his fate became as mysterious as Major Houghton's. Only in 1810 when Isako was dispatched to learn what had become of him, was the mystery partly solved. Apparently Park had got as far as Bussa; there, under attack, he had either been killed or drowned.

The journey had one pleasant interlude; he had stopped at Kamalia for a reunion with his good friend Karfa. As for the Niger, not until 1830 would its outlet be identified.

CHAPTER FIVE

BOY FROM BENIN

T HE NIGER'S outlet was one of those mysteries that becomes absurdly simple when the trick is explained. Ever since the days of Prince Henry, navigators had been making use of what Mungo Park had died in vain to find, but they didn't know it. They had no idea that what they called the Oil Rivers formed the mouth of the Niger. Approaching the Gulf of Benin, the river had built up a delta and made the rest of its way to the sea not as the majestic stream known to Sego and Timbuktu but as a series of lesser rivers—rather as an African empire under the stress of the slave trade waxed mighty and then broke up into petty principalities.

Inland of the Oil Rivers was an empire that suffered this fate, the kingdom of Benin. About the time Park was getting his first look at the Niger, a native of Benin was publishing an account of his exploration of the world of white men. The achievement of this African, called Olaudah Equiano by his own people, and Gustavus Vassa by the whites, was in a sense as remarkable as Mungo Park's, and his story of his own enslavement is an even rarer document than Park's journals. Many white men wrote of their travels in Africa, but the transplanted Africans who put their experiences on record may almost be counted on the fingers of one hand. Of these narratives, the one by the lad from Benin is the best.

It is a very different narrative from Park's, poorest in those details where Park is richest. An eleven-year-old boy kidnapped into slavery, Vassa carried no compass on his long and dolorous journey to the coast, and writing four decades later, he seldom remembered place names. He also lacked Park's trained scientist's eye—a fructifying moss would have left him where Wordsworth's primrose left Peter Bell. He even failed to record details that he could hardly have helped knowing, such as whether his own family were polygamous or whether human sacrifice were practiced in his community. Having adopted Christianity, he was probably reticent about such things. Where his narrative excels, however, is in the subjective experience of the impact of enslavement and his vivid impressions of details of the white man's ways that were commonplace to Park.

Vassa was born, he reports with the assurance of one who carries a birth certificate, in Essaka in 1745. The date is probably a reasonable deduction calculated from his age when he was captured, and the date of his reaching America. The "fruitful vale" of Essaka he places somewhere between the capital city of Benin and the borders of Abyssinia, an unhelpful bit of geographical fantasy best explained by the assumption that when he wrote he was looking at one of the old maps that represented Abyssinia as straddling the continent, almost to the west coast.

From Vassa's story of his journey to the coast, from what he says about the anchor-shaped medium of exchange used in Essaka, one may guess that it was in the park savannah country of what is modern Nigeria, probably south of the Benue and east of the Niger.

Whatever its location, Vassa's birthplace was so remote that its people had never heard of white men, and knew very little of their own gaudy capital, also called Benin. The town must have been not unlike Kamalia; apparently it acknowledged a kind of remote fealty to the King of Benin, but in practice it enjoyed local rule by its own elders. Vassa's father, the embranche or headman, was as respected as Karfa. He was no Moslem, however; Islam had not penetrated here.

Village life in Essaka was so similar to that in Israel in the days of the patriarchs that, looking back on it in his middle years, when he was well read in that most African document, the Pentateuch, Vassa wondered if his people were a lost tribe of Israel.

Something very like Levitical law prevailed in Essaka. Circumcision was performed soon after birth as among the Jews, instead of as an initiation rite at puberty as was the more common African practice. There were elaborate laws of purification, and a law of retaliation corresponding to the Mosaic "eye for an eye." The position of the domestic slaves was nearly as humane as that of the Israelite bondservants. Above all, the general mode of life was patriarchal: the father ruling his family, which apparently seldom included more than two wives, and being ruled in his turn in public matters by the elders, as in Israel in the days of the judges.

Even the dress was like that in Bible pictures, the men and women swathed in lengths of cotton which the women had spun and woven, the limbs of the girls and women weighed down with bracelets and anklets. What the children wore Vassa doesn't mention; probably they capered about in their own brown skins.

The houses in Essaka, except for the exotic thatch of their roofs, woven of palms fronds or of reeds, resembled those in sunbaked Bible lands. The walls were of red clay, daubed within with cow dung to discourage insects. The patriarch of the town had a day house (with the sides left open) and a night house; each wife was similarly provided, and there were separate huts for the slaves. Thus a single household, often surrounded by mud walls or moats, resembled a small village. The construction of the houses was simple, and each man was, as Vassa puts it, "his own architect." Neighbors clubbed together for a house raising, helping to build the walls and lift into position the roof frame. No one expected pay beyond the fun of singing while they worked and of sharing the feast later provided by the householder.

The custom in Essaka was for the man to eat apart from his women, waited on by whichever wife was officer of the day. Seats in the day house were logs, but there was often a bench for guests, and the room was perfumed with sweet-scented earth found in the neighborhood. In the night house, the sleeper lay on a raised platform of clay spread with a mat or skin, and fitted with cotton covering.

As was true everywhere in Africa, the children in Essaka felt closest to their mothers. "Strike me, but don't curse my mother," was a proverb among the Mandingoes. As a small boy, Vassa could not be induced to keep his distance from his mother even when she was "unclean" and sat apart in a little hut reserved for this part of the lunar cycle. He would run to embrace her, and so be caught with her in the taboo and presently undergo with her the rites of purification at the stream before rejoining polite society.

It was his mother who saw to his education, not only teaching him never to lie, the seemliness of washing before meals, but also the manly art of the javelin. She also taught him to honor the ancestral spirits before each meal by placing a small offering of food and drink on the floor. These spirits were always present, watching over every detail of the lives of their kin, punishing and rewarding according to merit. Sometimes Vassa accompanied his mother to the tomb of her beloved mother. The woman knelt before the hut, praying and weeping; Vassa stood trembling by her side. He trem-

bled because night deepened while she prayed, the spirits
became almost palpable, and even more so became the presence of beasts stirring in the bush.

There were livelier events. When the sun crossed the Line
there was a great jubilee and much noise making and elaborate dances in which everyone took part. Even the newborn
infant attended, riding his mother's back in the cradle sling,
and fathers, handsome as Othello in their long robes, engaged
the children, holding the smallest on a shoulder while they
took another by hand to teach him the footwork. Then there
was market day, not only a time to replenish household supplies, but also the best social event of the week and Vassa
trotted to market at his mother's heels.

It was there that he first got a look at the traders who were
to become important in his life. Essaka knew them as the
Oyo-Eboes, a people whose skin was mahogany red, who
went about the country to trade. Their barter included firearms, gunpowder, hats, beads, dried fish (a rare delicacy in
the uplands), and what they preferred to take in trade was
slaves. When there were none available, they settled for
lesser items, especially the sweet-scented earth peculiar to
the district.

The traders were mysterious people. Children wondered at
the enormous size of the bags they carried, and the elders of
the town kept an eye on their comings and goings, and would
not let them pass without inspecting their stock of slaves. But
this supervision was not strict enough, as Vassa was to learn
to his grief.

2.

Life was not wholly an idyll in Essaka. Little as its people
knew of the whites, they were under the relentless pressures
of the coastal trade. There were wars and rumors of wars;
their scale was petty and the enemies not necessarily from
outside Benin, but fellow countrymen at a remove. Essaka

was something like a frontier town. Its huts were fortified by a palisade of logs, sharpened at one end and tipped with poison. When the villagers went out to till the fields in the communal lands, they went in a body and carried weapons: muskets, javelins, broadswords, and shields large enough to shelter the whole body. In an attack, women fought with their men. Vassa's mother had come honestly by her knowledge of the javelin, and the boy had once watched from a tree while she fought with a broadsword.

In Vassa's time, Essaka was the victor. Captives were taken, the ringleaders put to death, and their followers enslaved. Some of the executions may have taken the form of human sacrifice, which was practiced so bloodily in the later days of Benin City. Vassa makes no direct mention of such sacrifices, but that they were much on his mind is obvious from his later narrative. He remembers among the trophies displayed in the marketplace the arm of a "virgin of note" slain in battle.

Fighting mothers and virgins notable in battle, were not rare in African history. In fact, the king of nearby Dahomey had a whole battalion of Amazons, as the Europeans called them, condemned to virginity because nominally they were the wives of kings who had practiced polygamy beyond all appetite or consideration for social welfare.

How often had Vassa's mother used her sword? Possibly only once, and that in the boy's early childhood. The incident lacks the graphic quality of his true memories, and has the sound of something a child recalls only because it has been told him so often. Peace was probably more common than war. Parents did not always take their children with them to the fields, but often left them behind to mind the compounds.

It was an uneasy peace, however. Armed invasion might be rare, but it was always well to keep a lookout for strangers skulking in the neighborhood. Once Vassa gave an alarm.

From yet another tree he saw unknown men spying on the children at play. At his shout, older children fell upon the intruders and managed to tie them fast until their parents could deal with them.

But Vassa couldn't always be in a treetop. One day when he and his sister had been left in the compound, their parents came home to find no one there. No one had seen the children go; no one had heard them cry. And no one in Essaka saw them again.

How did an African parent feel under such circumstances? How would Karfa have felt if he had returned to Kamalia to find that the little daughter he had put to school with Fantooma had been snatched away? How does an American parent feel when he finds a crib empty of even a ransom note?

When an African child dies his parents find comfort in tending the grave and in the rites releasing the little spirit into the solemn charge of its ancestors. The dead child remains a presence in the house. But how does one reach the spirit of a child who has gone no one knows where to a fate that none can picture? Attempts can be made. When the Africans began to realize the full impact of the slave trade and its kidnappings, some tribes added to their rites for the dead special prayers for the spirits of those lost in slavery.

But human anguish often demands more immediate appeasement. Behind the bitter little wars that tormented Africa in the century of the slave trade, there was often an incident like the disappearance of Vassa and his sister.

3.

The children had not seen the strangers at all. The first they knew, a woman and two men were already over the compound walls, pinioning them from behind, and gagging them so quickly that the whole incident was soundless.

The kidnappers knew the neighborhood. They had found a way through the bush well apart from the paths used by the villagers. They even knew a hut where they could spend the night and find provisions. But the children refused the food. They lay in each other's arms and wept.

Vassa and his sister had gone with their captors in the paralysis of will that one feels in a nightmare. But on the second day, when the strangers risked following one of the forest paths, the boy became alert. He thought he knew this way, and when he saw in the distance what he thought was a friend, he shrieked for help.

Then Vassa learned the use of the great sacks that the Oyo-Eboes carried with them. He was bound and gagged and thrust into one, his sister into the other. When the wayfarer passed by, he saw only three ordinary traders carrying their merchandise on their backs. That a chief's children were the merchandise he had no way of knowing.

The traders continued their journey, and when Vassa came out of his sack, he marked the direction in which they traveled, always to the setting sun. They trudged on for days, and then the children were robbed of their last comfort: they lost each other. They were still probably no great distance from Essaka, and the kidnappers, fearing pursuit, may have separated them to make identification more difficult. The children wept and pleaded frantically, but the sister was taken by one road and Vassa, so desolate that he refused food, by another.

They met once again, some time later in a house where Vassa and his master had stopped for the night. In the meantime the kidnappers had turned over both children to more respectable traders, and when the latter saw the tearful joy with which the children embraced, even they were moved. They allowed them to spend the night together, clasping hands across the belly of the man "to whom I supposed we both belonged," who lay between them. But this was their last meeting, though they never stopped looking for each other and hoping. Once, years later, Vassa thought he had

found his sister. It was in Gibraltar, and if Gibraltar seems
like an improbable place to find her, it was an equally improbable place to find young Vassa, but he nevertheless got
there. The girl, who looked very much like his sister, was not
even from his country.

The abductors of the children were not in the class of
slatees whom Mungo Park knew, respectable traders who
got their slaves by legal means; they were probably not even
respectable Oyo-Eboes. They were of a gangster class, and
their practice was the crime that the British called "trepan-
ning," one punishable among the Africans by death or enslavement. They were well organized; Vassa made note of
regular stages on their journey where shelter and provisions
were ready for them. But being outlaws, they could not take
their captives openly to the coast, and their art lay in passing their prey from hand to hand until it was indistinguishable from slaves legally acquired. During this process Vassa
fell into the hands of some respectable traders. Though Karfa
would never have admitted kidnappers to his coffle, he may
have carried their victims. His tragic Nealee might have been
such a one as Vassa's sister.

Vassa himself was ultimately destined for the coast. But it
took him six months to get there, and before he made it, he
had changed masters many times and passed through "many
nations."

4.

Capture and slavery are different things. Vassa did not feel
himself a slave until he was sold to a goldsmith who wanted
a boy to help him in his smithy.

It was not the work that bore in upon the lad the humiliation of his condition; his labors were not onerous. He was
often free to play with his master's children, and the wives
(one of whom was very like his mother), were kind to him.
What galled Vassa, who had been born a chief's son, was the

distinction drawn at mealtime, oddly anticipating custom in a land he was yet to see—he was segregated. While his playmates ate with their mothers, he ate apart with his fellow slaves.

It was this consequential triviality that made the general similarity of the village to his own intensify his homesickness. Essaka, he reasoned, could not be far away. If he watched for his chance to escape, fortified himself with provisions, and walked steadily into the rising sun, he would soon be home. Vassa took every opportunity to verify this impression. In the evenings he walked with the maidens to the spring to help them fetch their pots and calabashes of water so that he could innocently inquire, observe, and plan his flight.

A quarrel with a fellow slave, the elderly cook, prematurely precipitated his escape. One day Vassa killed one of her chickens; he hadn't intended to, the fowl had merely got in the way of a stone he happened to be throwing—a distinction that any small boy the world over would understand. But the cook was not a small boy. When Vassa, remembering his mother's strictures against lying, acknowledged having thrown the stone, such was her fury and his reluctance to take a thrashing that he hid in the bush, and when the day passed without his being found, decided to start his journey forthwith.

By nightfall, however, his resolution was shaken. He had not eaten all day, and it was hard to think of setting out without food. Moreover, searchers had passed his thicket, and he had gathered from their remarks that home was a much greater distance and in a more devious direction than he had imagined.

When night came and the village fell asleep, Vassa nerved himself to set out. But never had the dark been so full of jungle noises, distant roars, nearer rustlings, diabolical croakings. It was an hour when even Mungo Park, who had a naturalist's skill in distinguishing between noises, would have taken to a tree if he had no better shelter. The boy fought a losing battle with his panic. If lions and leopards let him by, what of the serpents? If these let him pass unharmed, what of the tall red Eboes with their sacks? Worst of all, if he set out in the dark, how could he find his way to the rising sun?

When the old cook came to her kitchen next morning to light her fire, she found what she hardly expected, a small boy who had wept himself asleep among the ashes of her hearth. Her anger had spent itself. She was kind and master was kind though the latter was apparently disinclined to keep a potential runaway and not long after the little slave was sold again and resumed his desolate journey.

The fact that the goldsmith could without ceremony sell Vassa indicates that the lad ranked as a "foreign slave," even though all the villagers spoke his own tongue and seemed to have heard of Essaka. It was far away, however, and although Vassa must have told of his kidnapping, a crime everywhere abhorred, even the powerful kingdom of Benin lacked the organization to restore the child to his people. If there were any village alliances to forestall and punish such crimes, they could have operated only in limited areas. The idea of returning Vassa to Essaka never occurred to the goldsmith, who had legal title to the boy, probably from a respectable trader. The child's earlier history was simply irrelevant, and need one believe it? Lads his age are full of yarns about being chief's sons and about red men carrying big bags.

5.

Now after his stay with the goldsmith came a journey so long that the exhausted Vassa often had to be carried on the shoulders of one of his guards. Did it take him beyond the confines of Benin? No way of knowing, but probably not; all that he remembered in later life was that the way led "through many dreary wastes, amidst the hideous roaring of the wild beasts," and that the apparent direction—it seems rather odd—lay to "the left of the sun's rising."

Presently he stopped at one of the few towns to which he gave a name. He called it Timnah, which might suggest the Gold Coast or even Sierra Leone, though the route he described could have got him to neither place. Wherever Timnah was, it was in beautiful country, with coconut groves shading the houses and sugar cane growing in the fields. Vassa sampled both products and found them good, and for the first time he felt a sense of homecoming.

A wealthy widow of Timnah saw him at the home of a merchant and took him as companion to her own son. Here Vassa was slave no more and even lorded it over the widow's boy, who doted on him and deferred to him as the superior in age. Far from being made to eat with the slaves, slaves were assigned to bathe him and perfume him and wait on him when he sat down to eat with his playmate. Day and night the boys were inseparable, sleeping on one mat, cosseted by the widow, who seemed equally fond of them both. Homesickness never intruded here; if his stay had been long enough Vassa might have forgotten Essaka, his mother, forgotten even his unhappy sister. But it lasted only two months.

Suddenly, inexplicably, as is the way of life in slavery, he was on the road again. One morning while his chum was still asleep, someone came for him and took him away. It was like being "trepanned" again. Had he in fact been kidnapped? Or had the widow taken him merely as a loan from the merchant? It is significant that Vassa knew what price the latter had paid for him—172 cowries—but was ignorant of any such arrangement with the widow. Perhaps the merchant had left him with her until the passing of the rains made it possible to send the boy on to the coast. Vassa makes no mention of seasons, but in the six months he estimates that it took him to reach the coast from Essaka, there had to be an alterna-

tion of dries and rains. Whatever the explanation, he was off
again, and doubly bereft.

For the first time he came among people whose speech
and manners were fundamentally different from his. No one
washed before eating, the men had not been circumcised,
and the women immodestly ate, drank, and slept with the
men. So far as he could tell, they propitiated neither gods nor
ancestors with offerings. They cooked in iron pots whose size
alarmed him, scarified their bodies, filed their teeth to a
point, and proposed to do the same with his. This the boy
resisted with success, and brutish as these people seemed,
their ways with him were not brutal.

In this uncouth company the boy came to a river whose
size astounded him. Hitherto he had seen no body of water
larger than a pond or the little streams that ran through the
coconut groves of Timnah. Was he only now, after so long a
journey, coming to the Niger?

The nameless stream became his roadway. To his terror
the lad was put into a great dugout canoe and paddled downstream in a convoy of canoes. At night the paddlers dragged
their craft ashore, built a fire, made a tent "of the shape of
a little house" with the mats they carried, and settled for the
night. Sometimes they bathed in a fashion as alarming as all
their customs. Like most upland people, Vassa knew nothing
of swimming. He sat on the bank and watched with enormous, incredulous eyes while men and women dived into the
water and swam about, boisterously shouting and splashing.

They went on. Sometimes the boy was allowed to leave the
canoes and was taken overland through tangles of forest. He
changed hands again and again, met new people, heard new
tongues. He took note of the country through which they
passed, particularly the rich soils where pumpkins, plantains,
and yams were abundant and "of incredible size. Even the
cotton grew wild and there was plenty of redwood." Did he
mean mahogany? Society was agricultural; if there were

mechanics, he noted none after the goldsmith of his first stop. Though he saw no warfare, people lived at the ready; as in his own country, both men and women "trained in the arts of war."

Suddenly there was an end of Africa. The travelers came to a water so broad that there was no sighting its further bank. It was turbulent, and came rolling and crashing up the sands of the beach, bringing tongues of white foam almost to the roots of the bending palms before they sucked noisily back.

It was not his first sight of the Atlantic that the lad remembered later. He didn't even recall being carried on stout shoulders through the surf, dumped aboard one of the great seagoing canoes and ridden on a swaying course. What etched itself on his memory was the "hollow place" that stood offshore. It might have been an island with trees naked of foliage and with a sharply geometrical design growing out of it. Sometimes he lost sight of the island as the canoe sank in a trough, but when the canoe mounted the next wave he saw it again, ominously nearer. The canoeists laid aside their paddles and reached out to lay hold of ropes that were being thrown to them. Somehow Vassa was heaved up a ladder and thrust over the bulwarks into the "hollow place."

Men with "horrible looks" fell upon him immediately, handling him roughly and tossing him from hand to hand. Vassa had thought the dark men who filed their teeth were outlandish; these he thought were not men at all, but spirits, bad spirits. They had long lank hair and faces which, whether jaundiced yellow or raw red, had a fundamental pallor, like something found on the underside of a rock.

When they released him, all breathless, he saw recognizable human beings. The deck was crowded with black people of all nations who were in subjugation to the specters. They sat in chains, bowed with grief, and the eyes of some of them were fixed on a great cauldron boiling over a fire. When the boy saw the cauldron, he knew everything. The alarming iron pots of the river people were nothing compared to this; it could serve only one purpose: to prepare human flesh for the feasting of these spirits.

The boy shrieked and fell to the deck in a faint.

CHAPTER SIX

IMMIGRANT SHIP

To VASSA the men with "the horrible looks" who now possessed him were spirits. Even when he gradually came to acknowledge them as a hitherto undiscovered species of man, it did not occur to him to collect the information which would in later life be his first inquiry, the name of their ship and its master. To the boy the "hollow place" was unique and needed no further designation; the crew wore one indistinguishable face, and he never raised his eyes to the captain.

For the sake of rounding out his picture and of supplementing Vassa's highly subjective account with objective detail, let us assign him a ship and a captain, the *Duke of Argyle,* commanded by a young Englishman John Newton. This ship was cruising the Guinea coast in 1751, a bit too early to include this lad in its cargo, assuming that Vassa estimated his dates correctly. But John Newton's ship will serve our purpose.

That the likes of Newton, who was both pious and virtuous, had command of a British slaver was proof that the occupation was, as he put it, "genteel." How should it not be? The *Duke*'s home port, Liverpool, was, thanks to its part in the slave trade, rising from a nondescript seacoast town to an immensely wealthy metropolis, and God would not have prospered it had He not approved. Besides, as the devout well knew, the native African condition was so unvirtuous, so depraved, that any change was benficial to the Africans. Shipping them to America was manifestly the only hope of their soul's salvation.

Captain Newton, now twenty-six, had been following the sea since he was eleven, when he had made his first voyage with his father, captain of a merchantman. Some of his experiences had oddly paralleled young Vassa's. In 1744 he had been "kidnapped," that is impressed, into the Royal Navy on the *H.M.S. Harwich*. In 1745 he had been exchanged to the captain of the *Betsy*, a Guinea trader, who had let him enter the employ of one Clow, a disreputable character who had a small trading post on an island off Sierra Leone. Under Clow and Clow's mistress, whom Newton called P.I., he had undergone a year of virtual slavery.

Fortunately his father had influence, and a captain who had been asked to find him had run across him on the Plantane Islands, and taken him on his own slaver, the *Greyhound*. When the *Greyhound* got back to England in 1749, Newton became first mate on another slaver, the *Brownlee*. In 1750, now well versed in the Guinea trade, he had received his first command as captain of the *Duke of Argyle*.

The young captain had only recently come to salvation. Until the return voyage on the *Greyhound*, Newton had been a conspicuous sinner and a freethinker fond of devising blasphemies so lewd that they bothered superstitious fellow mariners who thought that though a man must curse, there were limits. But on the homeward voyage, during a storm that disabled and nearly sank the *Greyhound*, Newton heard himself crying, "God have mercy!" God replied and brought the ship safely to port. Profoundly impressed by the incident, and above all by the fact that he had in desperate plight turned spontaneously to God, Newton set to re-examining the scriptures. Before he next set sail he had become a devout Christian.

Pious masters were not unknown on slavers, but Newton's piety was so intense and he himself still so young that his men eyed him askance. On Sunday he regularly summoned them to divine service, and noting that many found the Book of Common Prayer incomprehensible, he gave some thought to devising a prayer book suited to the needs of the rough men who followed the sea. He did not, however, read prayers to his cargo, and Vassa would wait a long time to hear the Christian doctrine.

Newton's virtue was such that he was vigilant in keeping his crew from ravishing such comely African girls as were brought aboard, and guarded himself from temptation by abstaining from strong waters except as they were required for his stomach's sake. He was now a happily married man, and before leaving England he and his Mary had made a pact: each clear night they would look for the North Star (low on the horizon in these latitudes) in faith that by God's will their eyes would meet in heavenly rendezvous.

Newton filled his leisure with study. Off palm-fringed shores, oblivious of the chants of men paddling their canoes his way, he steeped himself in the Latin classics and the composition of Horatian verse. Later, when he became a clergyman, he would find that this exercise had given him the metrical foundation for the composition of such hymns as "Glorious Things of Thee Are Spoken" and "Safely Through Another Week."

And insatiably he wrote his wife. To her he confided a recent revelation: that of all human callings, that of the captain of a slave ship offered the best opportunity "for promoting the life of God in the soul."

It was a concept that would have stunned one wretched lad in the hold, for at this stage Vassa had his own ideas of what the dreadful white men called God.

2.

The *Duke of Argyle*, a snow or brigantine of about 100 tons, had left Liverpool August 11, 1750, with thirty men and officers. She was headed into what was known as the "white man's graveyard," and on her return October 7, 1751, would have aboard only sixteen of the original company. The discrepancy was not wholly due to mortality; the young captain's reading from the prayerbook had not quelled disorderly impulses among his crew, and he had traded two recalcitrants to a passing man o' war. Others, however, had succumbed to fever and dysentery, among them the carpenter and the doctor, the latter being the only man aboard with whom he could enjoy intelligent conversation. Luckily their work was largely done before they died.

The carpenter's job was to prepare the ship to receive its human cargo. Soon after they passed Goree Island, off modern Dakar, he set to work in earnest. Barriers were erected in the hold to divide it into three "apartments," for the men, the manboys, and the women respectively; shelves were built in these compartments so that the captives could lie in tiers, one above the other, and barriers were raised to keep them away from the deck.

These barricades were the ship's protection against one great hazard of the trade, slave insurrection. Such was the dread of this event that the nearest ship would come to the aid of any ship in trouble, no matter what their respective nationalities. Portuguese, French, Dutch, and English were now competing on this coast and had no more natural affection for each other than the African Yorubas had for the Ibos or the Ashanti for the Mandingoes, but in such an emergency they made common cause.

Thanks to African ignorance of deep-sea navigation, an effective uprising could take place only off the immediate coast, where the fugitives had a chance to swim for it or could cut the cables to let the ship drift ashore. Successful organization for an insurrection depended on there being enough people aboard of the same tribe, or at least acquainted with each other's language. On a later trip Newton was to be threatened by such "mutinies" and as punishment for the threat put the leaders in thumbscrews. However, on this voyage of the *Duke* he was hard put to make a cargo; it came to him piecemeal, much of it, to his annoyance, very young—if he did not have Vassa aboard, he did have a number of Vassa-like "manboys." Such a young cargo never found the means to rebel.

Trading was carried on in two ways by a free-lance slaver like the *Duke,* as opposed to company ships visiting the slave pens at their own "factories." A mate was sent ashore in the longboat to follow the streams inland and conduct direct negotiations; on Newton's previous trip as first mate, he had had this experience. Canoes also came offshore to meet the ship, in fair weather whole fleets of them, their oarsmen chanting as they thrust forward on their oars, their muscular nakedness splendid in the sun. At ship's side they laid hold of the ropes, and one or two of them climbed up to the deck to dicker. At waterside the canoes jostled each other in the swells, and when a deal was made and merchandise was swung down from the decks, they jockeyed for position, each trying to seize the load for his own craft. Often in the jostling, butter, lumber, and rum went overboard, and the men leaped after them and heaved them into their canoes.

The canoeists along Sierra Leone and what was to become Liberia were often the Kroomen, a hearty, hard-working coastal people, seldom taken in slavery, who had early learned to profit by white men's needs by furnishing labor for the loading and unloading of their ships. They still do, in 1963.

Trade was reckoned in "bars," which during the slave trade replaced the native cowrie. A bar was merely a system of evaluation: so many units of iron, so many muskets, so many rounds of powder and shot, so many bolts of cloth. Its value was highly variable; the coast at large had no standard of weights and measures, and Newton laboriously translated his bars into pounds and pence.

By 1751 African traders had long since become sophisticated in their demands. Gone was the day, if it had ever been, when a prime slave could be purchased for a bright scarf and a handful of beads. The Africans wanted hardware, including European iron, which was cheaper than what they could manufacture for themselves; they wanted rum; they wanted cloth by the bolt. Gewgaws like beads and bells and pewter and mirrors were still acceptable, but only as added to the solid wares, or better still, as a gift, a "dash."

The slave ships also made neighborly calls upon white folk scattered along the coast, broaching a hogshead of rum for settlers who wanted it retail—two gallons for a Miss Webb, nine for Hannah Smith, a barrel of cider for a Mrs. Small who had a girl slave to offer in exchange. Were there so many lone Englishwomen along the coast, and by what chance had they come?

During his trip to Africa in 1751 Newton looked up two old acquaintances in the Plantane Islands off Sierra Leone; "old friends" was not his word for his former master, Clow, and Clow's mistress P.I. He well remembered how P.I. had resented him, had set him to menial tasks, fed him only scraps from her plate, and how when he fell ill of fever had refused him the charity of fresh water. Nor had Clow been kinder. Newton had indeed served his time as an African slave, and a foreign slave at that, unprotected by the safeguards set about the domestic slaves by African tradition. But the Plantanes, long since corrupted by the slave trade, had forgotten

African tradition.

Now Newton had the pleasure of presenting himself to P.I. and the unsavory Clow in the full glory of his captaincy. "I am as absolute in my small domain (life and death excepted) as any potentate in Europe," he wrote his wife. "If I say to one, 'Come,' he comes; if to another, 'Go,' he flies. If I order one person to do something, perhaps three or four will be ambitious of a share in the service. No man on the ship must eat his dinner till I please to give him leave; nay, nobody dares to say it is twelve or eight o'clock in my hearing till I think proper to say so first."

From the height of such dignity Newton could receive a visit from P.I. with affable condescension; he had the impression that she was ashamed.

But trade at this time was difficult. He approached Sierra Leone in heavy weather, running into a series of squalls and sometimes fog, when he couldn't see the coast, though he heard the surf ominously near. For all his bragging about the deference of his men, they made trouble. One tried to strike him in the presence of P.I.; others were disgruntled with their rations of rum and helped themselves from the stores, replacing what they took with water. He had to put some, including his unpopular boatswain into irons, releasing them not because this measure had induced sweet reasonableness of spirit, but because slaves were coming aboard and it did not do for Africans to observe that white men could also be chained.

(Vassa did observe such details, and they confirmed him in his conviction that he had come among altogether desperate savages.)

The slaves were coming slowly and Newton was often dissatisfied with their quality. The demand in America was for prime slaves, chiefly men, who could be put to work at once in the fields. Instead the longboat brought back to the *Duke* more undersized girls and boys than men. Newton measured the former: "two small girls, one of three feet, the other of three feet four inches." He got one woman "with a very bad mouth." He refused a "long-breasted woman." This type, called "fallen-breasted" in America, was unpopular for aesthetic and practical reasons. In the British West Indies, where many agents and overseers took Negro mistresses as a matter of course, fallen-breasted women lacked personal appeal. The fallen breast was also an indication of age, for it characterized women who had carried several children through the long African nursing period and who might well be past twenty-five, the cut-off age for prime Negroes.

Rats overran Newton's ship, damaging not only the stores but the sails. "We cannot get a cat on any terms, and those we brought from England have been dead for some time." The sailors fell ill, and even Newton, accustomed as he was to the coast, had one bout of fever. The infection spread to the cargo.

An epidemic among the slaves could turn any ship into a pest ship, and it was feared even more than insurrection. One captain, caught in this situation in the mid-Atlantic, took the precaution of dumping overboard all the seriously ill; he might have got away with this had he not charged his losses to the underwriters, who investigated and got the true story from his crew.

Such a recourse would not have occurred to the upright Newton, but while his ship lay off the African coast, he did try to stave off disaster by setting sick slaves ashore. "Put a boy on shoar, No 27, being very bad with the flux. . . . Sent a girl ill of the flux, No 92, on shoar to Peter Freeman, not so much in hopes of recovery (for I fear she is past it) as to free the ship of a nuisance." The girl died; the nuisance continued.

His crew was afflicted. He had to order immediate burial of the body of Edward Lawson, "being extreamly offensive"; carpenter Andrew Corrigal suffered ten days "of a nervous fever," died, and was buried "at daylight." Mr. Bridson, the mate, died, the doctor sickened and was sent ashore "to try if change of air and dyet will recover him from his flux." So many were sick that "am afraid shall not be able to keep the boats going."

With and without the aid of the doctor, who made a temporary recovery, Newton did his best to bring health to his ship. After the death of "a fine woman, No 11 . . . taken with a lethargic disorder which they seldom recover from," he had the rooms scraped, "then smoked the ship with tar, tobacco and brimstone for two hours, afterwards washed with vinegar." When the flux or dysentery spread among the Africans, he tried a change of diet: rice twice a day instead of the English provisions of beans and pease. "A little time will show wheather it agrees with them better."

Newton was learning, and on his third and last voyage with a new ship, the *African*, he would achieve a prodigy, an entire voyage without loss of life. But his experience on the *Duke of Argyle* was more characteristic.

3.

Vassa had perhaps come aboard while the slave quarters were being fumigated, since so many men sat on deck, bowed with grief, staring at the cauldron, whose size so terrified Vassa that he fainted.

The African traders who had brought him aboard applied themselves to reviving him and then to assuring him that the cauldron was not designed for the purpose he supposed. He was not to be cooked and eaten by these "men with horrible looks." A sailor brought him a mug of spirits, but Vassa shrank back from the frightening white hand. Only when an African held the mug to his lips would he sip from it, and then he choked convulsively. Palm wine he had known in Essaka, but not firewater.

The traders shrugged their shoulders, and climbed down the ropes to their canoe, leaving him to his fate.

Miserable as he was on deck, Vassa found conditions infinitely worse when he was sent below. No seaman, however hardened, could go 'tween decks on a slaver without nausea. One ship owner, advising a captain to set up a lazaret for ailing slaves in the forecastle, made the matter-of-fact observation that a physician trying to examine a patient in the hold would faint, or at best his candle would go out for lack of air. The place would have been hell in any climate—so near the equator it was a refinement on hell. The boy retched from the stench when he first went below and then lay weeping, longing to die. When sailors brought him food, he would just shudder. They had to drag him back to deck and thrash him before they could force it into his mouth.

When Vassa was allowed to lie on deck and breathe clean air, he looked for the first time at the water. The sheer mass of it appalled him; then presently he thought of leaping into it. But there were nets to prevent this, and when he studied the nets looking for an opening, the sailors drove him back.

With the passing of the days his spirit gradually grew quieter. He watched the cauldron simmering on the fire on deck; he saw horse beans put into it and corn and rice, but never human flesh. Among the men chained on deck were some from his own country whose dialect he could understand. When they assured him that slaves would not be killed, but would be carried across the water to work for the white men, he began to believe them.

"Have they a country besides this hollow place?" asked the boy. "How comes it then that in all our country we have never heard of them?"

"It is so far," said the men.

"Where are their women? Do they have women like ourselves? Why do we not see them?"

"They left them behind," said his friends, and then tried to explain how this hollow place, the ship, could be made to go. It had something to do with cloth which the white men hung on their masts with ropes "and then the vessel went on;

and the white men had some spell or magic they put in the water to stop the vessel."

The boy was incredulous until he saw for himself another ship come by in full sail and then magically stop.

Only spirits could work such magic—he was in a world of evil spirits. Until now, even as a foreign slave in Africa, he had seen little of human brutality. Here for the first time in his life Vassa had been thrashed; other slaves were whipped even more cruelly, and the white men even turned on each other. He saw them tie one of their own to a mast and flog him until he died and then cast his body into the sea.

Watching the cruel spirits work their spells, he found new cause for fear. Cannibals they might not be, but such strong magic could not be worked without offerings and sacrifices, and when sacrifice was required, who would be a likelier choice than he? This thought did not easily leave him. Two voyages later, for the boy who came late in childhood to the sea was to travel much of it, he was still obsessed. When that ship came across a group of grampus whales, Vassa supposed that they were kings of the sea coming to claim suitable offering by way of dash. By that time he had a smattering of English, and the crew, aware of his fears, took advantage. The sea kings, they told him, would not be appeased by the sacrifice of a skinny little African; they demanded someone fatter, and a lad somewhat older than Vassa had been chosen. From then until landfall Vassa never woke in the morning without anxiously reaching out to touch the boy beside him, who was his friend.

However, that was a later episode, and Vassa had come a long way in more ways than one—the friend who slept beside him was white.

4.

Vassa was not allowed to watch the crew work the magic of setting sail for America. The order to put everything below not wanted on deck included the human cargo. Vassa did not yet rank as a "manboy." Perhaps rather small for his age, in any case worn out by the hardships of the long trip to the coast, Vassa and other small children were stowed with the women. From that "apartment" he knew of the casting off only by the trampling and shouting on the deck overhead and the shrieking of the women as they felt the ship move out and roll with the swells.

The hold was not an observation post. True, there were some advantages in being with the women, who were not so often chained as the men. But they lay in close confinement in suffocating heat that made their naked bodies slippery with sweat. From the "necessary tubs" rose an unspeakable stench, and sometimes small children, groping in the dark, fell into them headlong. People began to sicken and die, carried off in Vassa's opinion by the sheer reek.

Once the ship was safely on course and far from sight of Africa, life became more bearable. In fair weather many slaves were permitted to spend much of the day on deck. The women were brought up and assigned homely tasks like cleaning rice and grinding corn for cakes. The sun felt good on their backs, the air was clean. The sea had flattened out, and they could even take pleasure in the sparkle and the blue of the water if they did not reflect on how much of it there was. Absorbed in familiar tasks, they could almost imagine themselves in their own compounds.

Vassa soon had the run of the ship. He had been so ill 'tween decks that he was brought up early and allowed to remain on deck for most of the voyage. Guardedly, he began to accept kindness from the crew.

The sailors were a rough lot. Well-bred Englishmen, whose nation was now becoming mistress of the seas through the sullen efforts of such men, considered them scum. Their lives on shipboard were also rough, as Newton well knew. As a disobedient midshipman on the *Harwich*, he had undergone the torture and the humiliation of being flogged on his naked back before the entire company and then cast into the cockpit, where conditions were not sweeter than the 'tween decks of a slaver.

In fact, on a slaver the sailors' lot could be worse than that of the slaves. Often they had no better sleeping quarters in all weathers than the deck. Their rations were sometimes more meager than those given to the slaves. Vassa shuddered to see them whipped—further evidence of the malignity of the white men.

But for all their roughness and their hardships there was often kindness among them, especially when they got away from the pestilential Guinea coast and into the familiar routines of the open sea. Like lonely GI's in far countries, the sailors on the slaver often made much of the children, making them little presents, instructing them to spit with the wind, even outfitting them in their own cast-off caps and jackets. Ship's officers, sometimes notoriously, gave special attention to the slaves that were included in their privilege. These were slaves of their own purchase who were transported with the rest of the cargo. One fourteen-year-old lad, the captain's "privilege" on another ship, traveled first class in the captain's cabin.

Another child took pride in serving his master and sharing his name. This was Venture Smith, named Smith for his master and Venture because he represented his master's "venture," or investment. Having a kind master gave him a sense of belonging. He probably lorded it over others, who like Vassa, were merely part of the cargo. So firm and undivided was his loyalty that when he was taken to his master's home in Connecticut he caused trouble: young Venture required education before he would take orders from anyone else.

However, Vassa was nobody's boy—though some of the women did what they could for him—and mostly he kept his distance from the crew. But when a sailor offered to let him look through a quadrant he did not refuse. Through it he saw clouds which looked like land, "which disappeared as they passed along. This heightened my wonder and I was now more persuaded than ever that I was in another world and that everything about me was magic." Even creatures of the sea shared the magic; he saw fishes that flew.

5.

The slavers were the principal immigrant ships to America in the eighteenth century, but they carried no William Bradford, no John Winthrop to record the emotional experiences of the immigrants. One has only the rare testimonies of the likes of Vassa and Venture Smith, both set down much later in life when many details had been forgotten. A pity that Mungo Park didn't record his experience on the *Charleston* as faithfully as he did his African adventures. As ship's physician, he had intimate contact with the passengers, and he spoke their language; his observations would have been priceless.

Daily entries were made in the ship's log by the captain or the first mate, and hundreds of these logs have survived, but they record only the practical matters. When a slave found a way through the nets and leaped overboard, the loss was noted, and sometimes the cause, such as that one man was delirious with the pain of dysentery or that another, "a meager man slave who was with the manboys in the middle room," could not be induced to grab the rope thrown to him. The logs say this much, but apparently not even the deeply religious Newton, who reflected every hour on the beauty of holiness and the miracle of his soul's salvation, gave thought to his African charges as having souls at all. That would occur to him much later in life, when he retired from the sea, took holy orders, and composed a hymnbook in collaboration with that "stricken deer," his friend William Cowper. Having at long last become an abolitionist, Newton looked back on his youthful occupation with stunned horror.

However, in 1751, to the master of the *Duke of Argyle,* the Africans were so much cargo. Such an attitude, maintained with little conscious rationalization, was indispensable to any sensitive man who proposed to stay with the trade. "I'm only doing a job," a slaver's officer would reply to a reproach, just as an American overseer, challenged in his use of the lash would retort, "I'm only trying to make a crop."

There was plenty to the job of sailing a slaver. The cargo, like any other, had to be delivered in good condition, and highly perishable merchandise like this demanded the closest attention. In some ways these involuntary immigrants got more care than the voluntary sort on more conventional immigrant ships, whose masters, having collected the fare, could be indifferent as to whether the passengers ate or starved, lived or died.

However, the slaves had to be fed regularly, force-fed if necessary; their quarters had to be inspected daily if only to insure that the living did not lie chained to the noxious dead. The slaves had to be brought to deck not only for this purpose and for the benefits of fresh air, but so that their quarters could be cleaned. On deck they had to be guarded. 'Tween decks, members of the crew with reluctant stomachs had to be made to do a thorough job of coping with what some regarded as willful nastiness. The tubs had to be emptied, the whole place scraped and swabbed, and if mats had been provided for the slave quarters, it was time to replace them and throw the used ones overboard—quickly.

On deck an attempt was made to clean up the slaves. Vassa recalled that women helped him bathe. And the nearer a ship came to its American landfall, the greater the emphasis was on personal cleanliness and smart appearance. The crew was set to barbering both men and women, shaving off infested tangles of hair and oiling the bodies that they might come smooth and sleek into market.

In American ports there was a further opportunity to freshen up. Charleston, South Carolina, had long ago learned from disastrous epidemics of smallpox and yellow fever to set up quarantine on Sullivan's Island until the cargo could pass health inspection. There were advantages in this delay. The captain could get to town to fetch back fresh meat for "the slaves and the people," and in fair weather the slaves could be landed on the island, given one last barbering, and made to walk about to relieve the cramps in their legs. This exercise was important, for the best of prime slaves would not command a good price if they came to market unable to stand upright.

Vassa's first port in 1756 was Barbados. If his ship stopped first in quarantine, he didn't know what was going on. What he later vividly remembered was that when it anchored at Bridgetown, planters swarmed aboard to inspect the slaves, make them jump, prod the firmness of their flesh, and try to communicate their destiny by pointing to the land. All that the planters' gestures achieved was panic among the newcomers. Though Vassa and his fellow slaves had been assured by their shipmates that the white men were no cannibals, they were now convinced that they were to be taken ashore to be eaten "by these ugly men." In their terror they stampeded, and even when they were driven below, they remained in such a turbulence of misery that seasoned Africans had to be sent for and brought aboard to explain to the newcomers what would be expected of them on the plantations.

After that they landed quietly enough, though everyone was confused by the strangeness of Bridgetown, a place unlike anything in Africa. They saw no familiar thatch; instead the houses were of brick, and storied, rising to what seemed to them tremendous heights. When a man came riding his horse to market, they marveled and conjectured whether this were one beast or two, and had their answer when the man dismounted.

It was given only to the hearty and one small boy to marvel so, and that not for long. They had not been invited here as sightseers; there was work for them to do.

CHAPTER SEVEN

MARKETPLACE

Vassa was the freer to look about him at Bridgetown because almost no one looked at him. Those who did turned impatiently away, for this was no lad to set to full- or even quarter-task work. At best he could serve with the grass gang, and any planter had enough children, aged folk, and pregnant women for that job.

Because he had made the voyage not with the "manboys" but with the young children in the "female apartments," Vassa must have been either small for his age or younger than he supposed. The long journey to the coast and on board the ship had been hard on him; no amount of oiling and sprucing could give him the appearance of a likely lad, nearly ready to take his place in the fields.

If he had landed first in Charleston, a port he was to know later, the local agent of a Rhode Island firm would not have brought him to the marketplace but would have set him aside among the "culls." This agent was a short, swarthy Huguenot named Henry Laurens. When a company ship came in, he met it at quarantine, partly to deter the captain from concealing evidence of pestilence or from cheating the underwriters and endangering public health by throwing dead slaves into the harbor, and partly to appraise the cargo before he advertised it for sale.

Laurens was often displeased with what he found. He had charged his captains to bring "likely, healthy people . . . men eighteen to twenty-five, women fourteen to eighteen. . . . Our people like tall slaves and strong withal." What he often got were runts, and "the most mangy creatures that ever were seen . . . a most scabby flock, all of them full of cockeraws, several with extreme sore eyes . . . very young children." He found Guinea worms, he found near blindness, and once a lad who was deaf and dumb. "They all seem to be proper subjects for the almshouse."

If the comment sounded brutal, Laurens' choler was directed at the captains, with whom he was engaged in a running feud. The culls he would treat with what kindness he could, putting the ailing into the slave quarters of a physician, setting aside the children until they could be fattened a bit. He was constantly enraged at evidence of cruel treatment on the ships. Tirelessly he instructed the captains to deal humanely with their charges, and he viewed with impotent fury the manifest disregard of such orders.

His voice did not carry to the Guinea coast, however, where the captains coped with problems which he, who had never been there, perhaps did not appreciate. They could see no reason why they should not flog an unruly slave as mercilessly as they flogged an insubordinate seaman; after a slave insurrection, even Newton had no qualms about applying thumbscrews. The trade was by its very nature unmerciful, and in spite of fat profits (Laurens got ten percent of whatever was cleared on a cargo) he would eventually withdraw from this occupation, genteel though it was.

In the meantime, having completed the culling, having set aside some prime slaves for his own estates in South Carolina and Georgia (he was scrupulous about not taking too many, lest he drive down the price of the rest), Laurens announced the time and place of the slave sale, either on the ship itself or at the marketplace, when the buyers would have their turn to inspect. This procedure was the same in Charleston, Savannah, or in the Sugar Islands, where young Vassa was getting his first impression of America.

2.

Experienced planters knew what they wanted and what to look for among the slaves. Occasionally a planter looking into the faces of the Africans recognized with a start of sympathy "the anguish and poignance of civilized men." But such impressions were rare. They were looking not at faces but at bodies. These they must study closely, for with "salt water Negroes" it was *caveat emptor;* they were warranted only against small pox. Even a man of fine physique might harbor an incipient ailment that would carry him off before so much as a day's work could be got out of him. Appearance could be illusory, the result of sleeking the slave with Florentine oil. It was also wise to make careful examination of a close cropped head, for shaving made gray hairs less visible.

Up to a point some disabilities, like "dropsy," could be disregarded. Owing to the long confinement 'tween decks and the weight of the chains, most grown men came from the ship with swollen limbs, and some with faces so puffed that their eyes were nearly shut. Unsightly as the condition was, it would pass; only extreme cases were to be avoided, especially if there were marks of chains that had pressed on the neck, for this sort of dropsy could affect the constitution.

Yaws, sore eyes were not desirable, or bad cases of the flux. As with dropsy, few slaves came off the ships entirely free of it, but a shrewd buyer made careful note how often a prospective purchase visited the "conveniences" placed in the corners of the yard. Too much coming and going was a bad sign.

So every buyer made his own medical inspection. He would open a mouth to examine the teeth, remove a shirt—even though the cargo usually left Africa in nakedness, it had been clothed in "Negro cloth" as it approached cooler latitudes—to inspect the musculature of the back and look for marks of the lash, which could be the sign of a "mean Negro." Women were disrobed to check for fallen breasts. Some of the slaves were made to run and jump. Children, who usually had the run of the ship, and most women could pass this test, but the men often stumbled.

In considering the nationalities available, buyers were variously motivated. Laurens' clientele preferred people from the Gold and Windward Coasts, and above all the Gambia. Mandingoes, known as "the gentlemen of Africa," were particularly popular. Angolas were accepted with more reluctance, and people from the Cameroons and Calabar were shunned on the grounds that they were suicide-prone.

There were other considerations. A planter who had had good luck with Ibos, hoped for more. Both kindness and expediency prompted some planters to look for fellow tribesmen of those they already possessed, for they would be happier among their own people, and the newcomers could adjust more readily with countrymen who spoke their language. Often these planters brought a seasoned slave to market as interpreter.

Others, though retaining their preferences and prejudices, preferred to mix the breeds of their slaves. They were fearful of adding more Ashantis or Pawpaws to those they had already, lest they enable the slaves old and new to "make a head" against their masters, either in outright rebellion or in "marooning" into the mountains and swamps. Some masters wanted their slaves to have no common language at all, and ordered them taught only enough English to enable them to follow the simplest directions.

Having made his choice, the buyer negotiated with the broker for terms. As of 1755 in Charleston he would pay £40 for a prime slave, assuming that the ship had arrived in a season when the man could be put to work at once. (Another of Laurens' quarrels with the captains was their coming in January, when in South Carolina the demand for labor was least, and buyers, having amiably viewed the cargo, would go home to wait for the price to come down.) Some slaves were sold under a lot system—a child and an "aged man," demonstrably past thirty, were thrown in at reduced price with a prime hand.

The terms were cash; that at least was what the brokers wanted. But since planters were always waiting on the sale of their crops, sugar in the islands, indigo, rice or cotton in Carolina, there often had to be a compromise: as much cash as could be got out of the buyer at the time, plus credit, and preferably not more than three months to pay the balance (with Laurens never more than six). Laurens considered this exigence a favor to the planters themselves, who in good times, when no wars threatened their markets, were notoriously optimistic and willing to overstock their plantations and mortgage themselves for years ahead in order to take their pick of a likely cargo. For to the planters the slaves represented much more than brute hands sweating in the fields: their labor would bring blooded horses for the racecourse, silver plate and fine china for the table, vintage wines for the cellars, silks and real lace for their daughters to wear when they were presented to the marriage market at Charleston Assembly. They meant a life of gentle manners and a career that might land the planter in the governor's chair.

3.

In Bridgetown, Barbados, in 1756, drums were beaten to signal that the sale was on, when Gustavus Vassa stood in the marketplace with the rest of the slaves. However, when the buyers went home, he was still there. No one wanted him.

Children were not a bad buy for a planter willing to wait for returns on his investment. They were a safer risk than adults, less subject than their elders to suicide or running away. Given kind treatment they adapted themselves quickly, often formed pathetically loyal attachments to their masters and took pride in ready response to training.

Sometimes planters were moved by compassion to purchase the very young. "They must have been kidnapped. No parent would sell such children!" exclaimed one West Indian planter when he saw a pair probably very like Vassa and his lost sister. He entrusted them to a slave family on his estate and rejoiced paternally to see how the children grew and flourished.

But the buyers in this market in Bridgetown were all business; what they wanted was stature and sinew, and Vassa was puny and malnourished. No one was perceptive enough to surmise that he had extraordinary staying power and acute intelligence. They ignored him, and Vassa was lucky, for had he been settled forthwith in Barbados, he would have missed a remarkable career, and most important, his freedom.

However, he didn't feel lucky. One by one he had seen his friends from the ship, including the women who had mothered him, taken away, leaving him forlorn. But he was not alone, for there were half a dozen other culls who were not salable, as he put it, "because of much fretting." Presently they were all bundled aboard a sloop and put to sea again.

After the voyage on the slaver this trip was almost a pleasure cruise. Far from being chained and herded below decks, the slaves rode as passengers, were on comradely terms with the crew, and ate "plenty of rice and fat salt pork." Suddenly Vassa was not only comforted, but an utterly happy boy. To him the seaways ran in only two directions: from Africa to the white man's country and back again. He had been to the land of the white men and now the direction of the ship could only be toward Africa. Having found no use for him, the white men were sending him home.

Sitting at the taffrail on a coil of rope, his eyes on shimmering horizons, the boy gave himself to a glorious day dream. He would be taken first to the coast, then to Essaka. One day, very soon now (the sloop had already passed islands that looked African), he would walk into the compound quite casually and surprise his mother. When she had finished exclaiming and weeping over him, she would lead him to his sister. For if the white men could find no use for a manboy like Vassa, what could they possibly do with her? There would be a feast for the whole village, and at it Vassa would perform like a singing man, recounting wonders.

Looking back on his experience, he now saw that it had been educational. At last he could warn the villagers of what merchandise the Oy-Eboes carried in their mysterious sacks. He would describe the life of the uncircumcised river people and their huge canoes. He would tell about the wonder of the illimitable sea, the fish that flew from it, the winged ships that sailed it. He would describe the white men still unknown in Essaka. And Vassa, insensibly adjusting himself to the ways of the white men on the little sloop, where manners were gentler than they had been, no longer thought of them as spirits or as "men with horrible looks." It is possible that he, who was to become a notable mariner, was already getting some grasp of the "spell" they cast on sails and anchor.

His anticipation of the tale he would unfold when he got back to Essaka was accurate. (It was exactly what happened when one of the rare African slaves permitted to make the round trip, a Fulani named Job ben Solomon, got back to his friends. Seized with an insatiable thirst for narration before he got to the town where his old father was waiting, he talked day after day, with the result that the old man died without seeing his son again.)

But there was one flaw in Vassa's reasoning: this sloop was

not bound for Africa. It seemed that the white men had other dwelling places than on Barbados. When their sloop headed into shore, it passed not mangrove swamps and palm groves, but the white dunes of the Virginia capes, and came to a mooring in a river. Abruptly the little dreamer found himself all soul alone, for the men who had been on the sloop with him were disposed of at once. With their departure Vassa was left speechless in a world where no one knew a word he said.

He was put into the slave quarters of a riverside plantation, and by means of signs, given busywork to do. He passed his days in an aimless limbo, pulling grass and picking up stones. If he had fellow workers, if he was part of what West Indians called a grass gang, this detail escaped his later memory. The people in the slave quarters looked like Africans, but they no longer behaved or talked that way. They may well have jeered at the uncouth ways of this "salt water Negro."

But in the Great House, with its white pillared verandas and its grove of shade trees, someone cast a compassionate eye on the bewildered child and sent for him. The master was ill, and Vassa was brought to the room where he lay and entrusted with the job of fanning him.

Fearfully the boy entered the house, and was not reassured when he passed a woman slave, the cook, who was loaded down with "iron machines," her jaws held fast in a muzzle, probably one of the contraptions designed to prevent "dirt eating." No explanation was given Vassa, who could only suppose that in this house a high premium was set on muteness. He entered the gentleman's chamber and, trembling, took up his work with the fan.

Only when the sick man fell asleep did Vassa summon the courage to lift his eyes to look about him. The room was full of "fine and curious furnishings," wonderful, but incomprehensible and therefore alarming. He saw and heard a "watch" ticking on the chimney piece, and having apparently learned another meaning for this English word during his travels, supposed that its function was literally to watch and report any misconduct on his part.

Then his eyes were caught by a portrait. It is remarkable that the child of a country where sculpture had reached a high degree of artistry but painting was unknown was able to grasp without instruction the one dimensional details of the portrait. What attracted him was the portrait's living eyes that met his and followed him implacably even when he shifted his position in an effort to break the spell. This must be another bit of magic, "some way the whites had to keep their great men alive when they were dead, and offer them libations as we used to do for our friendly spirits." But no African could expect good offices of a white spirit. When the sick master awoke and dismissed him, the boy went his way like one reprieved.

Thanks to the good food and cheerful life on the sloop, thanks to the euphoria of his brief day dream, however disappointing its outcome, the boy made a livelier appearance in Virginia than he had in Barbados. On one visit to the Big House, he was observed by Michael Henry Pascal, a former lieutenant of the Royal Navy, now in command of the *Industrious Bee*, which was loading with Virginia tobacco. Pascal took a fancy to the lad and inquired about his price. According to Vassa, who like many slaves took a natural interest in finding out how white men assessed his worth, his price was set at £30 or £40. Since such a price would then buy a prime slave, which Vassa was not, either he was mistaken, or Pascal had a prophetic vision of his qualities. In any case, Vassa was sold to Pascal and delivered to the *Industrious Bee* in the charge of an elderly black man, both riding one horse, a tremendous adventure for one who had so recently been unable to distinguish between man and beast.

On shipboard Vassa again hoped that he was bound for

Africa, especially as the crew told him so. However, it was a crew given to practical jokes, like talking of making human sacrifices to the "kings of the sea" when grampus whales and porpoises came alongside. Such talk frightened the boy terribly until he learned to recognize a joke.

It was on the *Industrious Bee* and from Pascal that he received his permanent name. Slave masters were fond of bestowing fanciful names on their slaves, like those of Greek gods; Pascal picked the founder of the Swedish dynasty. The boy had already been twice named, Michael on the slave ship, Jacob in Virginia, and he resisted this latest one. Though he was fast learning English, he pretended to be a dumb African whenever his master called "Gustavus." Pascal had to cuff him into submission.

His lessons in English came from a Virginia lad slightly older than he. Dick Baker was from a slave-owning family, but in spite of this, or perhaps because of it, boys being naturally eclectic in their companionships, he and Vassa became buddies. Thanks to Dick's instruction, when the ship put in at Falmouth and Vassa saw a most unafrican phenomenon, his first snowfall, he was able to ask questions and understand the answers. One morning he found the deck covered with what he took for salt, scooped up a handful and watched amazed as it vanished from his palm. He inquired of the first mate and shook his head at the answer—this story Essaka would never believe.

It was given him to pass the period of physical and psychological adjustment known as the "seasoning" in England. The climate may have been harder for him there, for he had one severe attack of chilblains and contracted small pox, but he was enormously compensated by the humanity of his treatment. He was brought with Dick into a private home and made one of the family.

After being surrounded by white people, their spectral coloring came to seem more natural than his own. At first he shrank from the women because they were too slender for African taste, and "they were not so modest and shame-faced as African women." He felt otherwise about a little girl in the household. One day he was struck by the rosiness of the child's face when her mother had finished washing it, and did his best to produce the same effect by a prolonged scrubbing of his own face. It was no use, and for the first time Vassa felt "mortified by the difference in our complections."

Nevertheless, he soon found an area where he might emulate the white people with more success. Dick and his master sometimes sat with small, box-shaped objects which they called books. Judging by the laborious movements of their lips, they were talking to them, and judging by the fact that they finished these seances with a new store of information, the books talked back. Vassa longed to talk to the books as "I thought they did and so learn how all things had a beginning." He watched his chance to get to a book in private, pose his questions, and then lay his ear to it to catch the reply. But the spell didn't work that way. Not until Pascal put to sea again, this time on the *Etna* of the Royal Navy, taking the boy with him, did Vassa find friends willing to spend the time to teach him both his letters and a bit of arithmetic. One shipmate gave him a Bible, and after exploring the Old Testament, the boy found what seemed to be a word-for-word description of life in his own Essaka.

While sailing on the *Etna*, Vassa really did get within sight of Africa, for he visited Gibraltar and there eagerly but vainly sought his sister He was now, or so he supposed, a full-fledged Englishman, and free as all Englishmen are. He was not.

His master had taken a new mistress who took a dislike to the boy, apparently because he did not disguise his preference for her predecessor. One day Pascal abruptly accused Vassa of planning to run away and sold him to the master of a ship bound for the West Indies. Vassa did not submit quietly to this; bitterly he reminded Pascal that he had been baptized in England, and that once baptized, an English slave could not be sold. It made no difference. Pascal got him aboard the ship, which sailed before the boy's shipmates could organize a rescue to save their friend.

In Montserrat he was sold again, for by now his energy and intelligence were manifest to the dullest eye.

CHAPTER EIGHT

THE SEASONING

THE RETURN to slavery was not the end of Vassa's story, else he would never have found the means to write it. His resilience would carry him through even this disaster, and we shall meet him again at the "freedom party" he gave to celebrate his emancipation, duly certified before legal authority.

But Vassa's is too special a case to stand for the general experience of the African immigrant. It is time now to trace the first days and first years in the new world of his ship-mates who were sold in Bridgetown market and moved at once to their new jobs. These people left no personal record; it was not given to transplanted Africans who remained permanently in bondage to compose autobiographies.

The record has to be patched together from bits and pieces, both from the West Indies and the American slave states. Documentation of the slaves' first experiences in the West Indies is more complete, and it is relevant. Not only were their earliest experiences similar in all British colonies, which at the time of Vassa's arrival included the American mainland, but many American slaves got what was called their seasoning in the islands. And South Carolina, important to this story, was founded largely by Barbadians, who brought their slaves and their slave code with them.

After the business in the Bridgetown marketplace was concluded, the new masters or their agents brought their purchases to their estates. It was recommended that this be done by easy stages, and if possible that the slaves ride rather than walk. In South Carolina, where the first plantations were along the tidal inlets, most slaves were probably transported in sloops or barges. Others had to be marched overland, stumbling on their cramped limbs, just as Mungo Park had watched the members of the slave coffle stumble and fall when they set out from Kamalia. For the slaves this was all drearily familiar.

It was also recommended that they not be set to hard labor until they had had time to adjust to the plantation. These recommendations came from H. Collins, who as a West Indian physician making regular calls on the "hot houses," as slave hospital quarters were called, had long and intimate knowledge of the difficulties of adjustment, and of the heavy mortality that attended the seasoning period, roughly the first two years. His advice was probably followed only when a slave was visibly ill. In Charleston, for example, planters would buy slaves only when sowing or harvest was imminent and the new hands could be put to work at once.

In the slave quarters the newcomers met their new companions. If these were later generation Africans, "Creoles" as they were called in Jamaica, or people as thoroughly cut off from Africa as if it had never been, the newcomers were often mocked and subjected to a kind of hazing. To the American-born they looked outlandish. They wore the meager clothes issued to them on the ship; their limbs were still swollen, and their faces bore "country marks." These, properly understood, were symbols of the dignity of African

manhood or womanhood, the incisions made on forehead
or cheeks at the time of their initiation, or in the case of the
"Mocoes" the filing of the teeth. The American-born slaves,
ignorant of African dignity, thought these marks uncouth,
and howled with derision.

Such rudeness would, however, be more characteristic of
later times. When Vassa came to America the slave trade
was approaching its height; the fact that mortality often
exceeded natural increase was forcing the owners of large
estates to replenish their stock regularly. "Creoles" were in a
minority, and those who remembered Africa crowded around
the newcomers in the hope of hearing news from home, of
finding one who spoke their tongue or perhaps even a kinsman. Against insuperable odds the African-born tried to
re-establish family ties on American soil. An African would
cling to a "brother," not because of consanguinity or even
co-nationality, but because he had been a shipmate, a fellow
veteran of the unspeakable experience on the slaver.

The first days at work on a plantation were bewildering.
The tasks were seldom wholly unfamiliar, but often the tools
were. In Africa the hoe had a shorter handle, and there were
no plows or wheelbarrows. A raw immigrant faced with the
latter gave it puzzled attention, and then removed the wheel
and hoisted the barrow to his head.

The expostulations of an overseer were no help. He delivered them in an exasperated shout, yielding to the common delusion that the English language, if shouted loudly
enough, is intelligible to any ear. Collins urged planters and
overseers to learn at least a few phrases of the tongue of
the newcomers if only for the sake of morale. Though large
estates often had a seasoned slave to serve as interpreter,
sometimes the nationalities of the recent arrivals were mixed
beyond any interpreter's resources. Under incomprehensible
orders the most docile slaves could give an appearance of
defiance, even when for their own peace of mind they most

earnestly strove to conform and please. Collins warned that punishment under such circumstances was senseless: the spirited would be rendered vicious, the gentle reduced to suicidal despondency.

But punishment there was, and harried overseers took early to the lash. Slavery, as Vassa remarked long before John Brown of Osawatomie thought he coined the phrase, was a state of war, and war is not waged by gentle persuasion. Those immediately in charge of the Africans, especially on estates managed by agents for absentee owners (almost universally the case in Jamaica) became brutal in the course of bending the wills of their charges to their purpose.

For example, in Maryland there was an African named Tony, who according to his master had no speech of any kind, "only an ugly yelling, brute beast-like." A stranger and alone in a world he never made, maddened by punishment for disregarding unintelligible commands, Tony took to running and hiding, watching his chance to steal meat from the smokehouse or hominy from the pot, eating "as ravenous as an hungry starved dog." When the overseers finally caught Tony, they tied him by the wrists to a ladder, his toes just touching the ground, and kept him so for hours to work the meanness out of him. When they cut him down, there was no more meanness in Tony—he was dead. Since there were witnesses, including a woman who had pleaded for him, the owner was put on trial. He was acquitted; after all, correction must be devised for the incorrigible. By what other means could one deal with a people who had never asked to come, had conspired bloody insurrection on shipboard and would conspire again in the new land?

However, there were owners who did try gentleness; there were idealists even among slaveholders. These fought a losing battle, because slavery as practiced on American soil was in the essence of things not an ideal condition. Even the humane Collins prescribed "terror to coerce [the slave's] obedience."

But he added, "Keep it always in mind that what you do . . .
is in violation of a positive right which no law of society can
effectively obliterate."

2.

The African-born clung to their own customs so far as
circumstances permitted. When they went to their intermin-
able labors, roughly from sunup to sundown, their first act
was, as in Africa, to build a fire at the edge of the field, and
by it, whatever the heat of the day, they gathered to enjoy
the respites of breakfast and dinner. Assigned to clearing
new land, some did as they would have done at home when
the dry season began by burning the brush. Of course this
practice was severely discouraged.

On festal days, such as the three usually allotted at Christmas, they reverted to whole-hearted paganism. The Christian
significance of this holy day eluded all but the few assigned
to duties in the Great House; despite all the pious talk of
redeeming African souls by transporting them to America,
in the early days of slavery very few Anglo-Americans be-
stirred themselves to this end. For the Negroes the holiday
was dedicated to the lord of misrule. They boldly invaded
the Great House to demand a dash, and spent their time
visiting and making as much noise as they pleased with
flutes, drums, and their own voices raised in song in unknown
tongues.

Authority did not interfere. The jovial uproar was proof
that the child-like Africans were happy in the condition to
which God and the slavers had called them. A quiet Christmas in the slave quarters would come in time to have ominous implications.

Some, such as the warlike Cormantines, went too far for
comfort. They discarded the hated work clothes of "Negro
cloth" or osnaburg, "a coarse kind of gray linen very much
like what bags are made of," and got themselves up in some-

thing resembling African costume. No records specified the details, except that they managed an alarmingly martial appearance.

In their quarters the newcomers practiced other Africanisms. In the West Indies, where the massive silk cotton tree grew as it had at home, they worshipped the tree. Once when an unbeliever threatened to cut down their fetish, the worshipers told him he would be struck dead for such impiety. He did cut it down but did not die, which shook their faith considerably. But they continued certain rites of witchcraft or "obeah" as it was called in Jamaica, and swore oaths over the blood of a cock.

Some followed the rites of the dead, burying their own with provisions and pipes of tobacco, and for want of separate burial huts, placed the dead under the earthen floors of their cabins. One Jamaica doctor, perplexed by a plague of dysentery, left the "hot house" to see what was going on in the cabins, and there he stumbled across the burial mounds.

There was a variation of the cult of the dead which authority was helpless to prevent. It arose spontaneously throughout America, from the islands to the mainland. Africans who could not endure the burden of homesickness found an infallible way of getting home. There had seemed to be no way at all. Unlike American Indians taken into slavery, who could watch their chance to escape to their own people, Africans acquainted with the breadth of the Atlantic saw no hope of crossing it. Yet there was one way.

On a Jamaica estate there was one night a distant sound of "mirth and gaiety." It was nothing unusual, so no one investigated, for at night the Africans were free, and they liked to go "night walking," especially if there was a moon. They visited and sang and played their flutes, and unless they did so too close to the quarters of an insomniac overseer, there was no objection. So the laughter aroused no curiosity, nor did the silence that ensued.

Only next morning, when at the sound of the conch shell a diminished labor force responded, did the overseer explore the grove from which the mirthful sounds had come. He had lost eleven prime hands, all Ibos; they were hanging by their necks from the trees. One had apparently acted as hangman for the others, and when his turn had come, two withes had snapped before he found one to bear his weight. The surviving Africans looked on with silent understanding—these men had gone home.

One master had found among his fresh imports a youth so personable in manner and appearance that he had taken him into service in his home. This was an unusual favor, for masters preferred "Creoles" about them.

But the wonders of the white man's house, which had so fascinated young Vassa, did not console this youth for what he had lost. He ran away. When he was found in the bush, desperately ill of dysentery, the master treated him with kindness and the youth gratefully responded. Unlike most Africans, who hated the "hot house" and often had to be forced to swallow the white man's potions, the youth took them gladly with manifest eagerness to get well. When his master ordered him a warm bath and issued a fine new suit of clothes, appropriate to the dignity of the Great House, the youth's pleasure was touching.

Next day, meticulously dressed, he was found hanging from a tree.

In his bewilderment the stricken master sought an explanation from the interpreter, to whom the situation was obvious. The youth wanted to go home; but first he had taken pains with his medicine and his dress because he would not return to his friends "in a sickly, ill-looking condition."

It was the faith of the Africans that a suicide was immediately returned to his own country. This belief had a kind of antiphonal response in Africa, where the rites for the dead now often included special prayers for those taken into

American slavery. In the new world the belief in "going home" was so prevalent among older slaves that this and not physical incapacity was the reason that few buyers would take an African over twenty-five. On the American mainland the desire to escape through suicide had some currency among free whites, who could be as homesick as Africans and sometimes adopted the African remedy. Editors in Massachusetts would inveigh against the "superstition" and the inconsiderateness of those who "left their stinking corpses hanging."

Suicides among Africans were most common in the first year of their slavery. In the second, the hazards were mostly of health, the respiratory diseases to which the African was subject even in a climate approximating his own, the agues and fevers that plagued him in the Carolina lowlands where he had to stand in water to cultivate the rice, the chigoes that ulcered his bare feet, and sometimes ailments brought in from Africa: a form of leprosy known in Jamaica as coco bay. Thus the first two years of slavery were attended with heavy mortality. The Africans who survived them might not live to ripe old age, but if sold, they could be certified as seasoned.

3.

After his experience in Gibraltar, Vassa gave up hope of seeing his sister again. By now he knew how wide the world was and how multiple the lands controlled by the white men. There was another consideration: in Gibraltar he had supposed himself free, but returned to America he found that he was still a slave. Had he come upon his sister there he would have experienced the supreme humiliation of the male slave—the inability to protect his womenfolk.

His new master in Montserrat profited by the youth's naval training and put him at work on his own trading vessels that plied among the islands and sometimes to American ports.

Often the ships carried newly arrived Africans; willy nilly
Vassa took part in the slave trade, and while serving aboard
these ships he observed the slave markets and saw what
could happen to young African girls in America. Helplessly
he watched the rape of mere children. With or without conscious intent, he abandoned his search for his sister—it was
better not to find her.

However, it is time to ask what did become of her, not for
Vassa's sake, but because her fate was to be crucial in the
development of America's most peculiar institution.

Possibly she was "Nancy, a very likely black Guinea
wench, speaks good English, very artful," who after serving a
term as house servant in South Carolina had disappeared.
She was believed to have taken advantage of her sound training at the washboard and sadiron to set up a business as a
laundress in the neighborhood of Charleston. When her
master advertised for her, she had been missing two years.

Perhaps her lot had fallen among the French in New Orleans, where she got her freedom legitimately and became
the C. Andrée who died in 1822, leaving an estate of
$2,090.99 and no known heirs. Apparently the court contem-
plated sending the money to her African kin, but she had
come "a great many years ago from the coast of Guinea as a
slave. . . . Neither her African name nor that of the tribe
to which she belonged could be ascertained."

If Louisiana had been her destination, she might have
been fortunate. There a pattern of racial amalgamation had
been set up by the early Spanish rulers, who, forbidden to
bring their wives along, took Negro mistresses and gave their
mulatto children a Christian education and established them
as freedmen. The French followed the same custom, and
though such alliances had no formal status, they had nearly
the same force as common law marriages, and in matters of
inheritance were so recognized.

White branches of such a family sometimes acknowledged

their Negro connection with pride, appreciating the fact that a Negro mistress had been a faithful and devoted wife who had wisely husbanded the estate with which she had been entrusted, and had brought up her children to be a credit to the community. Given such circumstances Vassa's grand nieces may have been presented at the famous quadroon Ball to properly accredited white men of New Orleans and so have made alliances worthy of a princess of the line, set up in handsome households of their own, with ample provisions for the support and education, often in France, of their children.

Vassa's sister may have been thus fortunate. It is not unlikely that the girl had the same intelligence and charm and ability to land on her feet as her brother. But it may not have so happened. After all, on his first arrival in Barbados, sick and cowed, Vassa had made no favorable impression. The chances are that the sister was set to work in a grass gang until she was strong enough to work in the fields. There her fate would have been very different.

She would go there day in and day out. The sacred taboos of her menstrual periods would be ignored. Inevitably she would mate and become pregnant, with small choice in the matter. Slavers to the British and American colonies brought in a heavy disproportion of males, and no nubile female could escape their attentions. The mating would take place without ritual, without payment of bride price; unless the girl were taken by one with power to defend an exclusive claim, a slave who served as driver for instance, she might not know who fathered her child.

In pregnancy her work would go on. If she protested, the overseer might have her lashed on the bare buttocks, first taking the precaution of having a hole dug to protect her belly, so that the contents, which represented negotiable property, should not be damaged.

Birth brought respite and brief joy. She would have a day

or two in the dubious comfort of the nursery, and when she returned to the field, her work would be light for a time and punctuated by intervals when an older child or the "Grandy" would bring her baby to the edge of the field, where she could rest by the fire and give suck. The living creature at her breast would be her first good comfort in her new life, the first thing that she could call her own.

Yet it was not hers. It was her master's, and he would want it quickly weaned so that her work could go from sun to sun without these interruptions. Remembering Africa, where weaning might not take place for three years, she would protest and weep, and the baby would add his voice to hers. But there would be no help for it. Sooner or later the child would be relegated to the care of the old Grandy in the nursery, and the intimacy of possession would be past.

In her second pregnancy Vassa's sister might induce the midwife to perform an abortion. West Indian doctors caught the midwives in the act of administering the "wild cassavia," which in the right dosage produced pains like cholera and evacuated the uterus. If she went full term, she might "overlay" or smother her child. This happened often on the American mainland where masters took it that the mother resented being bothered with the care of an infant. Other motives are on record: the mother of Nat Turner, herself daughter of an African, had contemplated that act rather than condemn another human soul to slavery.

To the slave children, growing up hit-or-miss like puppies, the mother often became a fading memory of early comfort and protection, while the father might not be even that. Sometimes the latter was white, the overseer, the master, or the master's son, who had slipped away from a commendable recitation with his tutor to an illicit rendezvous in the stables.

Under such pressures Vassa's sister and all her kind were being forced into polyandry and the chaotic beginnings of a matriarchy. By now memories of Essaka were dim, an echo of an almost unimaginable way of life. Was there a place in the world where women lived in "shamefaced" modesty, observing their taboos, fulfilling their purifications, cleaving to one man only, under pain of death for infidelity? The orderliness of African family life, now almost inconceivable to these women, could not be imparted to their children at all.

In 1703, too early to meet either Vassa or his sister, Francis Le Jau of the Society of the Propagation of the Gospel came to Carolina as a missionary, and was appalled at the depravity of the slaves, particularly the promiscuity of the women. He ascribed it to African original sin.

It was not. What he observed was the real crime of American slavery. It was not the brutality on slave ships or the hard life on the plantations; it was the nearly total destruction of that which was most sacred in African society, the family. It was the loss of a primal truth for want of which whole generations would fare the worse.

4.

In time ameliorations were brought about in the difficult life of the slaves, and some of these were due to the efforts of missionaries who at long last came to work on the plantations. Their accomplishments in America were on the whole more to their credit than their first efforts in Africa, at a much later date. There they were as a class blind to the delicately balanced intricacies of African tribal society, and without exploring the values of African religions, the missionaries dismissed them as "heathen." With the best of good intentions they sometimes did more harm than good, and Africans responded more readily to Moslem evangelists who respected such immemorial traditions as polygamy.

But in America the missionaries found a field white for the harvest. The African-born had no means of bequeathing their culture to their children. The son of an African would remember only his father's old country remedy for snake bite; African religions dwindled into obeah and voodoo, and occasionally the reverencing of a great tree. Children of immigrants are often ashamed of their parents' old country ways, and with children who often hardly knew who their parents were, this shame was reinforced by their masters' scorn for everything African. It was these American-born Africans who mocked the stumbling new arrivals from overseas. For them and their children, the ancient culture had been blotted out; living in a cultural vacuum, driven to mindless tasks, some of them were far closer to savagery than their ancestors had ever been.

The missionaries began slowly to fill the vacuum and restore some concept of the dignity of man.

They were not at first widely welcomed by the masters. A gentlewoman in Jamaica refused a Methodist minister's request to let her maidservant attend his chapel. "I need her for breeding," she said. Christian slaves were coming to an inconvenient insistence on Christian marriage in place of more casual unions. Christian girls sometimes rejected the advances of their overseers; some got wickedly beaten for this, there being no fury like that of an overseer scorned.

Le Jau, probably the first real American missionary, aside from colonial rectors who did have some house servants in their congregations, met similar resistance in South Carolina. A young gentleman said that he would never again come to Holy Table if his slaves were received there. A gentlewoman inquired in dismay, "Is it possible that any of my slaves could go to heaven, and must I see them there?"

This was in the early days of Carolina, barely two decades since the founding of Charleston. The profits to be made from rice and indigo had just been discovered, and since such crops required an expensive outlay for flooding and draining, large plantations and many hands were becoming the rule. Though Carolinians still made some unauthorized use of Indian labor (Le Jau's original interest had been the souls of these), the dependable labor force was African. Planters set to work the slaves they had brought from Barbados, and because the mortality rate was heavy in the rice fields, the planters imported replacements from Africa.

Le Jau seldom distinguished between African-born slaves and later generations, but that there were many of the former is attested to by the brutality he found among owners. He reported, "a poor slave woman . . . barbarously burnt alive . . . without any positive proof of the crime she was accused of, which was the burning of her master's house. Many masters cannot be persuaded that Negroes and Indians are otherwise than beasts, and use them as such." Male runaways were punished by castration and the women had their ears cropped.

Such masters were obviously afraid of the slaves, who were already outnumbering the white settlers. They saw them much as Prospero saw Caliban: crude, unteachable, watching their chance for rapine and rape. (Shakespeare, who could be large-minded about pigmentation in the skin of an aristocrat like Othello, may well have conceived Caliban from what he heard of African slavery.)

However, not all masters were barbarous, and Le Jau was permitted to teach the catechism to some slaves. He wrote to London for permission to baptize a slave who could not formally qualify. Le Jau knew none better for "sobriety, faithfulness, truth, and love of his master," but after twenty years in the colony this man could hardly make himself understood and "consequently cannot make such a formal confession of faith as is commonly requisite."

In contrast, Le Jau found another slave so forward that he could not only repeat the catechism, but learned to read the Bible for himself and took to prophecy. This frightened the missionary. It was not the man's conduct which worried Le Jau, for he was "a very sober and honest liver," but his fixation on the Book of Revelation. Le Jau began to hear more prophesying from other converts: "An angel came and spoke to the man; he had seen a hand that gave him a book." The preacher-slave warned his master of a judgment, and told him "abruptly that there would be a dismal time and the moon would be turned to blood, and there would be death and darkness."

Such prophecies anticipated those of Nat Turner, who a century later also read the Book of Revelation and led his people to bring blood and darkness to Virginia.

This local prophet's words presaged more immediate events: a devastating Indian massacre in 1714, and a few years later a bloody insurrection among the Stono slaves. Le Jau became as anxious as the masters about the wisdom of letting a slave learn to read. Ranging at will in the Bible, a slave ran across many inconvenient texts. Better that he sit quietly in church and heed the one text universally approved by slaveholders, "Slaves, obey your masters."

CHAPTER NINE

THE FREEDMEN

THE SUBJECT was delicate and it was critical. On July 10, 1766, when Vassa had undergone his second term of servitude for three and a half years, he braced himself to ask his master for his freedom. He had a friend to help him; the captain with whom he had been serving on his master's ships, took a fatherly interest in the youth and now volunteered to attend the negotiations.

Robert King had promised Vassa his freedom when he could produce his original purchase price of £40; he now had a total of £47 in his pocket, but as he well knew, the promise was not legally binding. Other masters in this situation had been known to up the price to the impossible figure of £300. Or they had simply refused, "You'll only go to the devil without me, you rascal."

Vassa had reason to believe that Robert King, a Quaker, would be bound by moral obligation. But he couldn't be sure, and he was grateful to his captain for offering to stand by. Even so, Vassa broached the subject fearfully, and his master's first words made his heart sink.

"What! Give you your freedom? Have you got £40 sterling? How did you get it?"

"Honestly," stammered Vassa, to which the captain added details, "that he knew I got the money honestly and with much industry, and that I was particularly careful."

"You get money much faster than I do," retorted King, and added that he would never have set such a price had he supposed that Vassa could raise it so soon. Painfully Vassa waited to hear that his price had risen, but his captain came to his aid.

"'Come, come,' said my worthy captain, clapping my master on the back. 'Come, Robert, I think you must let him have his freedom. You have laid your money out very well; you have received a good interest for it all this time, and here is now the principal at last. I know that Gustavus has earned you more than £100 a year, and he will save you money, as he will now serve you. Come, Robert, take the money.'"

And the money passed hands, actually not £40 sterling, but its equivalent, £70 in island currency. Vassa stammered his thanks and made for the Registry Office; even the payment would not insure his freedom until he had papers, signed, sealed, and delivered. But instead of fear, "all within my breast was tumult, wildness and delirium. My feet scarcely touched the ground, for they were winged. . . . Everyone I met I told my happiness and blazed about the virtue of my amiable master and captain."

The Registrar congratulated Vassa and took a guinea for his services, which he explained was half-price. King signed the papers, and the next day the Registry certified Vassa as "manumitted, emancipated, enfranchised, and set free."

For the first time since his kidnapping in Essaka, he was in legal possession of his own body. He clothed it in "Georgia superfine blue clothes," and then spent some of his remaining six pounds on parties for his friends. They were generous in their good wishes, and the new freedman was touched by "the blessings and prayers" of elderly slaves who did not begrudge him the good fortune that they could not hope for themselves. And being still very young, barely in his twenties by his reckoning, Vassa preened himself in his "Georgian superfine" before the coy attentions of "sable females who formerly stood aloof."

But no female could tempt Vassa to remain in Montserrat. He was bound for London as soon as he could work off a moral obligation of his own: to please his former master and his captain he reluctantly signed for two more voyages on the *Nancy*, this time for wages of thirty-six shillings a month. On the first of these voyages the good captain died, and Vassa, who had learned something of navigation, returned to port as acting captain of the *Nancy*. On the second, under new command, the ship was wrecked off Bahamas Banks, and when Vassa finally got back to Montserrat, he could not be persuaded to sign again.

It was too risky. Serving on coastal ships to the American mainland exposed the freedmen to constant hazard. Even in Philadelphia, where the Quakers tried to preserve human rights, he had seen a freeborn Bermuda Negro taken captive, his papers destroyed, and sold into slavery. Vassa himself had just escaped a similar experience in Georgia, and he would not risk again what had been so dearly bought. Early in 1767 he signed on as a hand on the London-bound *Andromache*.

Back in England Vassa looked up old acquaintances. Kind ladies wept over him, but Pascal only stared blankly.

"How," he asked, "did you get here?"

"On a ship."

"I supposed that you did not walk back to London on water," remarked Pascal dryly and turned his back. But Vassa was not through with him. He had a lecture to read his former master on his treachery to a faithful servant; he

had a demand: his share of the prize money to which he considered himself entitled for having served in naval engage-
ments. Curtly, Pascal said that there was no prize money and
that if there had been, he as master would have been entitled
to it all.

The ladies, shocked at the conduct of Pascal, who was
their cousin, helped Vassa arrange to apprentice himself to a
competent hairdresser. Long ago, while he was serving with
Pascal in the Navy he had learned something of the craft
from a shipmate. Now for six months he applied himself to
mastering it thoroughly, living on the thirty-seven guineas
he had saved and devoting his free evenings to receiving private instruction in the French horn and perfecting his arithmetic in an evening school. In February 1768 he entered the
employ of a gentleman in Pall Mall.

But the pay, only twelve pounds sterling a year, was disappointing, a scant third of what he had been earning as
seaman. So it was that Vassa found that he could not rest
from travel. He followed the sea again, at first avoiding any
ship bound for the perilous American ports, which he might
have called "the black man's graveyard." Eventually he got to
the Arctic on a polar exploration. It was the unlikeliest of
destinations for a boy born in Benin, though come to think of
it, when the pole was finally reached, an African was there.

2.

Vassa in England and in the Arctic is of no further interest
to this story, barring one episode late in his life. But one of
his earlier experiences is still relevant. How did he achieve
his purchase price? How did any slave manage to join the
small but slowly increasing body of American freedmen?

While he was serving with Pascal in the British Navy,
Vassa had learned the technique of the "venture," of invest-
ing in small wares for which there was a demand in foreign
ports. The principle of buying cheap and selling dear came

to him naturally; not for nothing had he in childhood accompanied his mother to market. African women were and still are accomplished merchants.

Vassa was so successful in his ventures that English ladies who befriended him entrusted him with ventures of their own. He had something in him of an African Dick Whittington, and by the time of this return to slavery had a nest egg substantial enough to have eased his way in buying his freedom; but the money was stolen.

In his first months at Montserrat, however, there had been no further opportunity for ventures. King had been impressed by the boy's intelligence, that he was literate and understood "arithmetic tolerably well, as far as the Rule of Three," so he promised to treat Vassa as no "common slave." Nevertheless, Vassa's first labors were pulling the oars of boats sent about the island to collect sugar and rum; sometimes his services were lent to other masters to help fit a vessel for the sea. Later Robert King set Vassa to work on his wharves as supercargo. Only much later did the master consent reluctantly to let him work as deckhand on a Bermuda sloop, and only then could Vassa resume his merchandising.

At the time his capital was a single half bit, threepence in English money. However, at St. Eustatius he invested this money in a glass tumbler which in Montserrat he sold for a whole bit. With this he bought two tumblers, and so it went until within a month Vassa's capital was a dollar. "I blessed the Lord that I was so rich."

Even such modest enterprises as these were not simple for a slave who had no rights that an unscrupulous white man need respect, especially when friends and protectors were at a distance. While his stock was still reckoned in "bits," and a pound sterling seemed impossibly remote, Vassa and a companion set forth in St. Croix to sell limes and oranges in which they had invested their whole capital, (twelve bits in Vassa's case). They had heard that there was demand for the fruit here, but they were hardly ashore before two white men took what the slaves offered for sale and went their way, laughing at pleas for payment.

An appeal to the commanding officer of the fort at St. Croix got them only the threat of a horsewhipping. Desperately they returned to the house of the white men and raised such a clamor at the door that presently Vassa's bag was returned to him. The other slave, an elderly man, pleaded in vain, so Vassa shared his fruit with him. For this good deed he was rewarded, for in the market his own share of the fruit brought thirty-seven bits.

Later on when he served on longer voyages, to Philadelphia, Charleston, and Savannah, Vassa's capital could be counted in pounds instead of pence. With an eye to the long view, he parted with a substantial sum of his money to induce the first mate to teach him navigation. For a slave this was an unprecedented request; along the American mainland slaves often served as common seamen and as river pilots, but to teach them navigation was strictly forbidden.

Not long after this, Vassa was involved in a crisis with his master, who had become suspicious that his prized slave would jump ship if offered further opportunity. Vassa had not lacked for invitations to do so, but had refused, partly because of loyalty to his master, and partly because of his disillusionment at the precarious existence of freedmen in America. Thanks to the captain's testimony about Vassa's punctual obedience, King's suspicions were assuaged. When Vassa was allowed to sail again, his master entrusted him with cargo of real value, tierces of rum and sugar, and agreed to give him part of the profit from the sale of these goods.

One of Vassa's last voyages brought him a series of mishaps. He had reached Charleston in the midst of the celebration of the repeal of the Stamp Act, and the city was alight with bonfires and resounded with the roar of cannons. This seemed like a good omen. But even though Vassa disposed of his stock readily enough, he could not get a fair price. One man refused payment outright for a puncheon of rum; only when his faithful friend the captain intervened would the man pay, and then only in copper dollars. Vassa took them perforce, but when he tried to exchange them in the market, he was roundly abused and threatened with a flogging for "offering to pass bad coin."

At Savannah, the next stop, he was nearly killed when he spent a Sabbath evening visiting the slave quarters of a Dr. Perkins. The latter objected to the presence of a strange Negro in his yard, had him badly beaten and thrown in jail. Again it was the captain who came to the rescue, but the episode ended Vassa's trading for some time.

On his last voyage, in 1766, both Vassa and his captain were about to make their fortunes. It was not merely the sale of merchandise, which this time went well, but the promises of a silversmith whom the captain knew, who offered great rewards for passage to the West Indies. The man fell ill before he could sail, so Vassa and the captain took turns nursing him; they were to be the heirs to the silversmith's fortune, which he kept in "a nest of trunks."

Despite all their care, the man did die. When Vassa and the captain eagerly searched his trunks, they found his store of wealth to be exactly $1.50, not enough to buy a coffin. "We went away greatly mortified and left the deceased to do as well as he could for himself, as we had taken so good care of him when alive for nothing."

It was not the most graceful of Vassa's exploits, but it was nearly his last as a slave. During a delay in this voyage—they were in Savannah again—he had "laid out above ten pounds of my money for a suit of superfine clothes, to dance in at my freedom." And the captain, after recovering from his ill humor at the perfidy of the dead silversmith, helped Vassa approach his master, so Vassa went dancing into freedom.

3.

In spite of Vassa's more unusual adventures, his way of obtaining freedom was the way many other slaves got theirs. There were still other ways, but many like Vassa accumulated capital little by little until they had the purchase price. Usually it took them much longer to do this than it had taken Vassa. Sometimes a slave, grown old in the process, renounced his own prospects in order to bequeath the money to his children.

Many slaves got money by marketing what they could find to sell. Few had the advantage of going from one port to another, but those who lived within range of a town could get permission to visit it on Sunday and display their wares in the marketplace. Some came from a distance to do this; in Jamaica, where Sunday market was an accepted custom, some slaves journeyed twenty-five miles, traveling most of Saturday night, and starting home after market closed towards noon. Others who lived near the coast, as on the tidewater plantations in Carolina, might get the use of their master's barge or construct a dugout of their own.

Some slaves sold handicrafts, such as baskets; fishermen sold their catch; others sold the produce from their own gardens, which they cultivated during dinner breaks, after working hours, and in their own released time—usually twenty-six half Saturdays a year. In the islands, where the slaves were expected to raise most of their own provisions, some masters considered this Saturday allowance excessive. In such a climate, so they said, a slave needed only one free day to raise all he needed. It was a contention that took no account of the aggressions of the tropical weed, which grew quite as luxuriantly as Guinea corn. Of course these masters never remarked why, in this case, the laborers had to put in such long hours on the master's crops.

The object in going to market was not necessarily to earn

enough money to buy freedom. Even adequately provisioned slaves hungered for the means to purchase variety for their diet, especially meat; and there were few so rough and ready as not to covet more presentable clothes than those fashioned from the annual distribution of "Negro cloth." The women wanted printed calicoes and white muslins; both men and women, even those who by preference went barefoot into the fields, wanted shoes for ceremonial occasions. The methodical, frugal Vassa, even before he was certain of his freedom, lavished an extravagant sum on those "Georgia superfines." Buying fine clothes was a more attainable end than buying freedom; yet not a few persevered until they had bought it.

Sometimes a slave could sell his labor for money to buy freedom. He could either work after hours, or by agreement with his master he could hire himself out on the understanding that beyond a given sum his wages would be his own. For a time this practice was fairly common in Carolina, and in Connecticut young Venture Smith earned his freedom by chopping wood. He became a prodigy with his ax, a John Henry, and having bought his own freedom, he did not rest. He also bought it for his wife, and in time for several of his friends in Colchester.

4.

In all such efforts the slave was dependent on two circumstances: his master's consent, and his master's willingness to respect the property rights of the slave.

Legally, the ascription of property rights to one who was chattel property was an anomaly. However, the slave's rights were formally recognized in the British West Indies, though only a few years before, emancipation was imposed by Parliament on the bitterly protesting colonials. (It was the year 1832, and the mainlander Americans were no longer colonials. If they had been what might have happened?)

As slave society became stabilized on a given plantation, the workers became tenacious of their rights to their own cabins, their sticks of furniture, and their garden plots. They even bequeathed their property to kinsmen, which under the African principle of the "extended family" could include any close friend. No passing of papers or any legal authority was involved in such transactions, but masters and overseers usually respected them. Trouble came only when the overseers tried to shift the slave quarters to different grounds. Even when the new choice had obvious advantages, being on high ground away from the periodic flooding of the lowlands and in closer proximity to the fields, slaves could resist removal with passion. They would not willingly leave what had become to them the homeplace.

Decent masters also respected the slave's right to his earnings, but of course not all masters were decent. Vassa knew one so mean that he confiscated without payment the fish that his slave had caught on his own time. "I can't go to anybody to be righted," the slave said to Vassa. "I must look to God Mighty in the top for right." Another who had served on shipboard had earned enough to buy a little boat of his own. When it was commandeered by a white man and the slave sought redress, he was "damned very heartily by his master, who asked him how dared any of his Negroes to have a boat."

Nevertheless, over the years, custom acknowledged the slave's right to such property as he could honestly amass. One North Carolina court passed on the claims of the heirs to the estate of James H. Martin to the sum of $143.97 belonging to a slave, who had earned the sum by working his cotton patch on his own time. They called the claim "ungracious and unfounded," and ruled that such "petty gains" came under the same heading as "the savings of a wife in housekeeping by sales of milk, butter, cheese, and vegetables."

Some gains were more than petty. A Jamaican cited the

extraordinary case of an efficient, highly regarded slave mill-wright who was in control, if not legal possession, of several slaves of his own, whose services he hired out at will. West Indians said that in a pinch they borrowed money from their more prosperous slaves.

All this was good business for the master, and an insurance against petty thievery. The slave who had nothing he could call his own seldom felt compunction about helping himself to his master's property, especially corn from the crib and meat from the smokehouse. As Frederick Douglass wryly remarked, recalling his boyhood slavery in Maryland, both slave and provision belonged to the master—theft was merely the shifting of the contents of one tub to another.

5.

There were other ways to freedom than the purchase of one's body. In Virginia until the middle of the seventeenth century, in New Netherlands while it remained under Dutch rule, the Negro servant got his freedom as the white indentured servant did, by serving out his term. When the first Africans came to the mainland, the nineteen "negars" bought in Virginia in 1619 from a Dutch man of war, the colonists knew nothing of chattel slavery and adopted no laws on the subject for two generations. Thus there were Virginia Negro families who could claim an older foothold in the country than the descendants of the *Mayflower* whose ancestors had never been slaves.

The change in the status of the Negro was caused by the discovery of the profits which could be made in single-crop farming, from the "sweet scented" tobacco in Virginia and Maryland. Such crops called for many hands and a more permanent labor force than one whose terms would presently expire. Slavery was the obvious method of holding a laborer to his job, and the African, marked by his color and too far from home to run back to it, was the obvious choice.

The Carolinas, founded later, started with single-crop

farming, and many Carolinians came from the Barbados with
both slaves and an established slave code. There was never
any nonsense in Carolina about indented service for Africans.

Even so, there were ways for a slave to prove his right to
freedom: the mixture of races, and legislation that gave the
child the status of his mother. Since the first Africans imported were males, they took what mates they could, occasionally a white woman servant but more often an Indian.
When Virginia formulated its laws on slavery, it exempted
the Indians with the result that the study of genealogy became popular among people of mixed descent. Those who
could trace their line to an Indian grandmother and prove it
in court could join the community of Virginia free Negroes.

Legislation never worked the other way, however, to give
the child the status of its father. If it had, once African
women came to these shores, the number of free Negroes
would have grown by arithmetic progression. Not every
white slave holder kept a Negro mistress, but there were
some who did, and the presence of young women on the
estate, "black but comely" was a temptation to their sons. Not
even the most vigilant tutors in the best families could deter
their charges from leaving a recitation in Virgil to sneak off
to the slave quarters.

Such adventures, supplemented by those of the overseers,
contributed to the rising birth rate. The mulatto children
seldom inherited favors; indeed the presence of outraged
wives or resentful half-brothers often made their state doubly
unfortunate. But there were exceptions: masters who without acknowledging relationship sent a child north to be educated, or provided for their manumission in their wills.

Not that all masters who freed their slaves were motivated
by secret kinship; with mistresses who did so it was probably almost never true. They were only rewarding good and
faithful servants. For some aging and lonely widowers,
widows, and spinsters, their "people" had long been their
only human companionship.

There was, for instance, George Wythe, famous Virginia jurist, who freed his slaves and in his will provided property for them. A protégé, Michael Brown, was to inherit his bank stock in equal share with a nephew, provided he lived to come of age. He did not, for the nephew, enraged by such sharing, visited the Wythe kitchen one morning and put poison into the coffee pot. His rival drank of it and died, as was the nephew's intention, and so, unfortunately, did his uncle, who came in unexpectedly to enjoy homely comforts in the kitchen. Wythe saw the dying agonies of young Michael, and when his own began and he got the story from the cook, he lived just long enough to disinherit the nephew. It was the latter's only punishment, for the cook was the sole witness, and it was the universal rule south of Delaware that the word of a Negro could not be taken in court against that of a white man. (Some legal opinion did hold that a slave's word might be accorded the same value as "the cry of an animal.")

The incident took place in 1806 when a wave of emancipation inspired by the egalitarian principles of the Declaration of Independence was finally subsiding. For a time, especially in Virginia, but not only there, wills regularly conferred freedom; and there was legislation freeing and honoring slaves who had fought in the Revolutionary War.

By the time of Wythe's death, the tide had turned. Virginia masters still bequeathed freedom to their slaves, but the latter could accept it only under painful, often impossible conditions. They must within the year leave their homes, their friends, or else they would be sold on the auction block.

Virginia had passed this law in 1803. South Carolina had passed even stricter restrictions on emancipation three years earlier. These changes had been caused by sensational events in the West Indies, for which the embarrassing assumptions set forth in Mr. Jefferson's Declaration were partly responsible.

CHAPTER TEN

TURNING POINT

I N THE 1790's it looked as if the American slave trade had come to an end, and as if slavery itself were on the way out.

The resumption of the Guinea trade after the Revolution had been desultory; only Georgia and North Carolina ports were now open to African immigration, and they would be closed by the turn of the century.

The abolition movement was respectable and was engaging the attention of both American and English intellectuals. A public had been created for the memoirs that Gustavus Vassa was composing and for Mungo Park's account of his travels. For the first time the general reader had authentic knowledge of the African way of life and of the viewpoint of the African slaves.

John Newton was also writing his memoirs; in affliction of spirit, for he had long since committed himself to abolition, he was recording those activities as captain of a slaver which in youth had filled him with pride.

In the northern tier of American states, emancipation was

the order of the day, either outright, as by the terms of the Massachusetts constitution of 1784, or gradually, as in Pennsylvania. This did not necessarily betoken any excess of virtue among Yankees; their merchants and sea captains had enjoyed the lion's share of the profits of the Guinea trade, and when the latter became forbidden by Federal law, many would become expert in smuggling contraband. Had New England soil favored the plantation system, good Puritans might have demonstrated even more ingenuity in finding Biblical sanction for slavery than the Southerners; but their soil was adapted to small farms, industry, and commerce in which slave labor was of small utility.

The year 1793 was an *anno mirabilis;* events then took place that would on the one hand extinguish Southern sentiment for emancipation and on the other demonstrate the validity of the Negro's claim to full citizenship. In the first category was an uprising in the French colony of San Domingo, of which more later, and the invention of a gadget by a young Yale graduate then living in Georgia to help his employers clean their cotton. The revolutionary consequences of Eli Whitney's cotton gin were not immediately apparent, but he might as well have invented the atomic bomb; better, indeed, since no one at the time would have known what to do with the bomb.

The other and happier event was the heroic action taken by a community of free Negroes in Philadelphia to prove themselves worthy of the full citizenship that the Pennsylvania constitution of 1780 had conferred on them.

2.

It was largely due to Quaker influence that Pennsylvania had committed herself to abolition. Long before the Revolution the incomparable diarist John Woolman had circulated the colonies north and south persuading Quaker slaveholders of the iniquity of keeping human souls in bondage.

His views were reinforced by many of the "Pennsylvania Dutch," especially by some Moravians. Originally settled in Georgia, the Moravians had the only colony founded with a ban on slavery, and they moved north when Georgia abandoned the ideals of its founders.

Thanks to such cause Pennsylvania, though bordering on the regions where slavery was firmly rooted, became the first state to provide for emancipation. It was a graduated plan; every child born to slave parents after the adoption of the constitution was to be free after he had undergone twenty-eight years of indentured servitude. Those born before 1780 were still slaves and their masters could, if they chose, sell them into states that had no such plans. However, the impulse that impelled the adoption of this law also impelled many masters to free the older slaves. And most remarkable of all, the manumitted were enfranchised; they were full citizens.

Throughout the South, Pennsylvania was to become the promised land. "I have heard that there is a place called Philadelphia where the black people are all free," said a South Carolina runaway, "but I do not know which way it lies." And the man to whom he spoke, Charles Ball, who had been kidnapped into slavery, would remember, and in his own breaks for freedom set his sights for Philadelphia.

The situation was, however, less than utopian. Enfranchisement had come by a legislative fluke, by inattention of those opposed to the fine print in the emancipatory statute; it would not last indefinitely. Masters who freed their slaves were not always nobly motivated; some were ridding themselves of the burden of supporting the aged and infirm. Even younger freedmen, cut off from the slave quarters without knowledge of a trade or any means of their own, were often at a loss in their new state.

The transition came most naturally for those who, like

Vassa, had earned their purchase price by habits of frugal industry, but even for them it was not always easy. Richard Allen of Philadelphia, now prosperous and on his way to becoming the first Negro bishop in the Methodist Church, had, like Venture Smith, blistered his hands cutting countless cords of wood to buy his freedom. He well remembered his blank misgiving when he finally achieved freedom, the sense of being rudely thrust from his father's house. He had floundered in a series of odd jobs before he found his way to that economic independence that alone gave freedom reality.

Now he was distressed at the number of freedmen in similar plight and worse. Some were becoming vagrants and beggars, going to their former masters' kitchens for handouts; some were continuing habits of petty thievery, which in slavery had seemed something like a moral obligation.

To cope with such problems, Allen and other Negro leaders, among them Absalom Jones, who like him had labored for his freedom, founded the Free African Society. In the tradition of the late Benjamin Franklin's multiple self-improvement groups, it was dedicated to teaching its members to guide their fellows to higher standards of morals and industry, and to providing modest financial aid for the really helpless.

In 1793, when the society was half a dozen years old, it received a call for help from the white community. An emergency had arisen which would give the freedmen "a noble opportunity . . . of manifesting their gratitude to the inhabitants of that city which first planned their emancipation and have since offered them so much protection and support as to place them in point of civil and religious privilege on a footing with the whites."

The ex-slaves met at once to give this appeal their prayerful consideration. It was a situation that called for prayer.

3.

Late in July 1793, a shipmaster had committed a public
nuisance by dumping a cargo of damaged coffee at the docks
at the foot of Water Street in Philadelphia. By August the
stuff had putrified and its effluvia was an annoyance and
worse to the neighborhood; it set off an epidemic of yellow
fever, which spread through the whole city.

Such was the best medical opinion as to the cause of what
quickly became a disaster. Dr. Benjamin Rush also noted
that the stricken bore little marks like inflamed mosquito
bites, and that though the summer was dry mosquitoes were
uncommonly abundant. But he made this observation only
as a coincidental curiosity.

By late August the city was in panic. The effect of the
constant tolling of the bells for the dead had become so
demoralizing that the City Council had forbidden them to
toll at all. Some physicians were fleeing the contagion, and
those who like Rush remained were so beleaguered that they
had to whip their horses to force their way through the
importunate who begged them to come to their families.
Rush's office was thronged. A man not given to emotion
would try to speak only to give way to uncontrollable sob-
bing; another would stare at him blankly, as if he had forgotten on what errand he had come.

There were not enough doctors, not enough nurses; there
were not enough of the able-bodied to bury the terrible
dead. In late August the crisis was such (though it would
not reach its peak until October) that Rush inserted an
appeal to the Negro population in the *American Daily Ad-
vertiser*. He called to them to provide nurses on the grounds
of civil responsibility and on the premise that as Negroes
they had natural immunity to the pestilence. It had not yet
appeared in the Negro quarters and another medical authority had written that "there is something very singular

in the constitution of the Negro which renders him not
subject to this fever."

There was some partial truth in this belief. It may be that
in Africa, where the disease was common, Africans had built
up something of the same immunity that Europeans had
against measles, and which minimized its effects when they
caught it. In a devastating visitation in Charleston in 1698,
at a time when Africans predominated among the Negroes,
the mortality from yellow fever had been chiefly limited to
the white masters. But there were now few Africans in
Philadelphia; the African ancestry of Richard Allen was so
remote that it would not have occurred to him to trace it.
He well knew that Negroes were not immune; there had
been a lesser epidemic in 1792 and 64 Negroes had died of it.

But danger could not exempt them from civic responsibility. Though the privileges of the Philadelphia freedmen
were not so great as Dr. Rush supposed, compared to those
of the slaves in the South they were enormous. And with all
the annoyances and inequities to which the freedmen were
still exposed, there were many Philadelphians like Rush, who
had signed the Declaration without making mental reserva-
tions that man's inalienable rights were conditioned by the
color of men's skins, people whose sense of loyalty and fair
play would enhearten Negro leaders through emergencies
more distressing in the long run than a mere natural catas-
trophe.

The Free African Society accepted the challenge.

By October Philadelphia was a city of the dead. President
George Washington had removed the government to Ger-
mantown, and everyone who could manage it had fled. Those
who remained went into the streets only on unavoidable
errands, shrinking from each other, holding cloths soaked in
vinegar to their noses, or sucking compulsively on pipes and
"seegars," since vinegar and tobacco were believed to have
efficacy against the plague. Otherwise only the dead moved

in the streets, often trundled to their graves unattended
except by the Negro who drove the dray.

Rush was stricken; he recovered, but his sister and three
of his pupils died. There were times when Allen and Jones,
who had got their education by prodigies of will power, and
had only the smattering of medicine that Rush had been
able to impart to them in a hurry, were nearly the only
physicians available. The myth of their immunity had been
exploded by the death of several nurses from the African
Society.

But the two lay physicians went their rounds, carrying
their lancets, their bottles of "ten and ten" as the compound
of calomel and jalop was called, carrying their Bibles—for
they also attended to the spiritual needs of their patients—
carrying with them printed instructions to be left in households where there was someone sufficiently in control of his
faculties to make use of them. And though they lived with
death, they went unscathed.

They came to houses where only the children were left
alive. "Mama's asleep. Don't waken her," whispered one
child, and wept wildly when, seeing that this sleeper would
not waken, they called the burial crew. They found orphans
wandering helplessly in the streets, comforted them and led
them to the orphans' home. No use to appeal to a neighbor
to take them in; most doors were bolted against anyone from
a house where disease had struck. They had seen parents
thrust by their own grown children into the street when they
so much as complained of a headache. They knew of a man
alone in semi-delirium who had wailed from his window
for hours before someone, a Negro, could be induced to
fetch him water.

Nurses, white as well as black, for the membership of the
African Society was not large enough to supply the city in
such a crisis, did what they could. Longfellow's Evangeline
made her rounds about this time. As the poet would pres-

ently report, she laid cool consecrated hands on fevered brows and culled fresh flowers to lay by their sickbeds. These were not the duties best remembered by the nurses from the African Society. What they knew was less suitable for celebration in dactylic hexameter: coping with uncontrollable hemorrhages and the stench of black vomit; scrubbing and changing and lifting; bolting the windows when they, singlehanded, found no other way to restrain a delirious patient. They would be left day and night without relief until they fainted from exhaustion and muddled their directions, unable to recall what they must do and what they must avoid.

Some would know that if they caught the contagion and called for help, members of the family who had been avoiding the sickroom would enter just long enough to grapple with them and force them into the street or an outhouse. Not that this always happened. Just as not all black nurses were equally brave and devoted, not all white folks were callous and ungrateful. Some families would turn to and nurse the nurses. But it wasn't possible to forget a nurse remembered only as Sampson, who had gone from house to house, refusing all pay, only to die in neglect when his time came.

The hardest task was the burial of the dead. Originally the African Society had not accepted this duty, and when Allen saw that no one else would undertake it, he called on volunteers. But the work was beyond their strength, and at first he could not find men to serve even for pay. Not only the dead but the beds they had died on had to be buried, and the work was feared more than nursing. Not until he offered 22/6 (at least $20 in modern currency) a day did he succeed in mustering a dependable crew of five.

The nurses served for six dollars a week; a few members of the Society would not accept pay at all. "I will not sell my life for money," said Caesar Crandall, a charter member. A young girl reasoned, "If I go for money God will see it and may make me take the disorder and die, but if I take no money, he may spare my life." It was a bargain, and God kept His end of it; but Crandall died.

In mid-October when the first frosts came, the epidemic fell off sharply. By November 9 Rush considered it over, and reckoned the dead since August 1 at 4,044, of whom 305 were Negroes, whose "peculiarity of constitution" had not protected them. He composed his narration of the disaster, not neglecting recognition of the valor of the nurses of the African Society.

But a Matthew Carey of the Mayors' Commission, a gentleman who had taken refuge in the country at the height of the epidemic and had its details at second hand, also wrote, and struck the members of the Society a blow in the face. He used phrases like "the vilest of the Negroes," and although he acknowledged civic virtue in leaders like Allen, he charged the Negro nurses with neglect, extortion, and pilfering.

Not all white people were so graceless. One family gratefully remembered an old woman, who when asked to set her wages, said, "Only a dinner, Master, on a cold day." Mary Scott, who refused to take more than fifty cents a day for nursing Richard Mason, was rewarded by his widow by a lifetime annuity of six pounds. But many people took it that Carey had written nothing but the truth. What better could have been expected of the shiftless freedmen?

In grief and anger Allen and Jones composed their own story; it is the most vivid picture of the calamity. They could not avoid a protest: "You try what you can to prevent our rising from the state of barbarism you represent us to be in. . . . If you love your children, if you love the God of love, clear your hands from slaves, burden not your children or country with them. . . . Will you, because you have reduced us to the unhappy condition our color is in, plead our incapacity for freedom, and our contented condition under oppression as a sufficient cause for keeping us under the yoke?"

They concluded with a sermon against bitterness, addressed to their fellows. "Let your conduct manifest your
gratitude toward the compassionate masters who have set
you free, and let no rancor or ill will lodge in your breast for
any bad treatment you may have received. . . . If you do,
you transgress against God, Who will not hold you guiltless.
He would not suffer it even in His beloved people Israel,
and can you think He will allow it with us?"

Thus in Philadelphia, especially in their churches, St.
Thomas Episcopal, where Jones was an unofficial rector, and
the Bethel Methodist which Allen was soon to found, the
leaders continued their struggle to bring the abundance of
life to their fellow freedmen, and a sense of fair play to
their late masters. Often their efforts seemed doomed by
the nature of things, yet in this city there were always men
like Rush, and there was always hope. There was not to be
in Philadelphia the violence that would come in South Carolina and Virginia, where by the end of the century it became
virtually impossible for a slave to become free.

4.

While the yellow fever raged in Philadelphia, far to the
south, in the first island discovered by Columbus, events
were leading to the establishment of Haiti, the first Negro
republic.

The movement had begun some years earlier in the demand of the island's free people of color that the principles
of liberty, equality, and fraternity of the new revolutionary
regime in France be interpreted to give them civil rights.
When their own legislature temporized in granting their
petition, they rose in arms. At this stage, there was no slave
insurrection, as was supposed on the mainland. Such slaves
as participated in the struggle were under orders from their
masters, both white and colored; some were fighting for the

Revolution, some against it.

Emancipation was not contemplated until after 1792 when the French National Convention sent three commissioners with a body of troops to restore order. At first the commissioners were helpless; it was only after a bloody massacre at Cape François in June 1793 that they sought allies by promising freedom to slaves who enlisted under the banner of the Republic. This promise, intended only as of local application, caused so much ferment among the slaves at large that the commissioners made it general. On August 27 they issued an emancipation proclamation; independently the National Convention abolished slavery throughout the French colonies.

The result was not at all what slave owners, American and West Indian, would have supposed; the ex-slaves remained quietly at work on their several plantations. Presently they were given new laws by which they could contract with a landowner to work by the year for a specified share of the produce, or by the month or the day for wages. They were no longer to come under the compulsion of the whip, and disputes were to be settled not by managerial fiat but by court. Under this system the island returned to prosperity, especially when Toussaint L'Ouverture rose to power, and the prosperity might have continued but for outside intervention.

For three years the British, acting on appeals from antirevolutionary French planters, tried to conquer the island; their efforts were vain and the British sustained greater losses than the islanders. The real crisis came after the turn of the century when Napoleon, misled in his turn by malcontent planters, sent an expedition to reimpose slavery. Toussaint L'Ouverture was captured by wile, and in 1803 French troops brought carnage and tremendous destruction to the island. This too was in vain; Haiti was a Napoleonic defeat. But the damage was irreparable. The profitable sugar cultivation was at an end, the machinery and even the canes having been destroyed. French planters lost their estates, for now they were expelled bodily from the island.

These events did not go unnoticed on the American mainland; South Carolina, whose ties were closer with the West Indies than with some of the northern states, was especially concerned. There was anxiety as French refugees arrived with frightening tales of bloodshed and devastation, which they attributed, inaccurately, to slave insurrection. South Carolina had had a taste of that in 1739 when the slave Cato had led a bloody revolt at Stono, and South Carolinians now took precaution against the spread of the infection. Later refugees were forbidden to bring their slaves with them, and lest their own slaves get subversive ideas from the Haitians already among them, South Carolina passed a law which in effect made emancipation impossible.

This was in 1800 when, as it happened, South Carolina was on the point of resuming the African slave trade. Thus it came about that just as a fresh influx of Africans, many of them imbued with the warrior tradition, was about to come to the country, it was ordained that in South Carolina they could have no hope of freedom unless they fought for it. As the Free African Society had done in a different context, they accepted the challenge.

CHAPTER ELEVEN

END OF THE RUN

CHARLESTON had long been the liveliest of ports. Against the charming backdrop of the city, the white steeples of St. Michael's and St. Philip's, the gracious homes with their stepped gables, the massing of the live oaks, there was always a cluster of masts at the waterfront. They belonged to the brigs and frigates and sloops that traded with the West Indies, London, and the North. They belonged to the lesser craft of the fishing fleet; they were supplemented by the scows in which proprietors of the plantations along the Ashley and Cooper Rivers sent their produce to port for trans-shipment. There were even the little dugouts of the slaves.

But for nearly three decades after the outbreak of the Revolution there were no Guineamen. Then suddenly, in 1803 they were back. Charleston was in the slave trade again, and the approaches to the harbor filled with craft from the Guinea coast, waiting their turn to land "live cargo" at quarantine on Sullivan's Island. And now there was an urgency in the business, especially in 1807, when time was running out. On January 1, 1808, the slave trade would be cut off forever by Federal law.

But for the protest of Georgia and South Carolina delegates, the prohibition would have gone into effect with the adoption of the Federal Constitution. The delegates had managed to insert a provision that the government not act in restraint of this trade for twenty years. Their efforts seemed superfluous. South Carolina had re-entered the trade only briefly, and Georgia, last of the importers, had closed her ports to African immigrants in 1798.

But as prospects grew that Congress would set a definitive cut-off date, South Carolina slave owners saw the wisdom of improving their stock with new blood while there was time. There were other reasons. Planters had been learning the efficacy of Eli Whitney's cotton gin, by virtue of which the South was acquiring a new and immensely profitable staple. In 1803 they saw the prospect of new virgin soil on which to grow their cotton; Mr. Jefferson had purchased the Louisiana territory from Napoleon in the same year that the latter undertook to reconquer Haiti. The clearing of new lands, the planting and cultivation of the new crops called for far more hands than could be got by natural increase.

To Africa was issued a second and pressing invitation to America, and the Africans came.

Again captains from Newport and Charleston raced each other to the Guinea coast, and competed for cargoes on a bullish market. Ships from Liverpool and London intensified the competition, for Parliament had adopted the same deadline as the United States Constitution for prohibiting slaving to the West Indies. By 1807 there was no time to take account of the finicky preferences and prejudices of the importers. Let the latter cry as they would for Negroes from the Gambia or Gold Coast as against the "Gullahs" from Angola, a captain who found small pickings in the preferred latitudes would cross the Line and ship on a cargo of Gullahs before it was too late. This was the time that the sea islands of South Carolina and Georgia got their notable Gullah population.

Some traders, tarrying too long in Africa, or delayed in passage by storms or lulls, never made it, and suffered the fate of so many Flying Dutchmen. At least three ships were caught, the *Amedie*, the *Africa*, the *Tartar*. The *Amedie*, missing its deadline, was captured by the British on its way to Cuba. The ship was judged the lawful prize of its captors; with the slaves, many of whom had languished and died in the senseless limbo of waiting, it was "he who endures shall be saved." The survivors were "freed to the sole use of his majesty."

In Charleston these were heady days. Such seasoned immigrants of earlier voyages as lived nearby watched their chance to paddle their dugouts to the ships at anchor, or visit the wharves and slave marts to look for fellow countrymen and get news from home. Many had natural access to the vessels, for Negro seamen, stewards, pilots, fishermen, and longshoremen, abounded on the South Carolina coast.

One man visited the *Cleopatra* in December 1807, and finding compatriots, conspired with them in a break for liberty. Residents in the outer parishes stared to see them go, nearly a dozen men and manboys, clad in red flannel jackets and blue nankeen trousers, none but their leader able to speak a word of English. Their flight was not immediately interrupted; they had managed to take with them half a dozen muskets.

This break for freedom, though abortive, was prophetic. So large an influx of Africans was to have a profound influence upon the Negroes of tidewater South Carolina. Arriving almost in a body in the short span of five years, they were received very differently by the "seasoned" Negroes than newcomers infiltrating more gradually.

House servants, who had absorbed something of their

masters' attitudes towards Africa as the "dark continent," where brutish savagery prevailed, and whose only ancestral tradition was that an African kinsman had talked gibberish when excited, might mock. But most newcomers were put to work in the fields, where manners were different.

In the early 1800's many South Carolinian Negroes retained some vestige of their African past. A manboy of fifteen imported by Henry Laurens just before the Revolution would still be only in his fifties by 1807. His memories of Africa might be blurred, but they were still there, and his contacts with Africans during the brisk trade of 1803–1807 would bring back what he had forgotten. The massive intrusion of vigorous young newcomers, many of whom, once past their seasoning, were not cowed at all, but fertile in plans for resistance, imbued in the slaves who had been in America for several generations a new respect for that which they had been taught to despise. The wave of immigration produced something like a renaissance of African culture, creating on American soil a continuity of tradition seldom observed outside the Sugar Islands and Brazil. The great thing was that now an exile could always find compatriots somewhere about.

Something else gradually dawned on Afro-American comprehension at this time. They were not a minority group; in the country they were many and their masters few. In South Carolina at large their numbers looked to be somewhat better than equally matched. It was a thought that gave food for reflection.

2.

Three nationalities stand out in this final immigration, each represented by a name that was to be written into South Carolina history a few years later.

The smallest group was probably the Senegalese. They had a notable representative in a man called Perault, whose

home had been a seven day journey from Goree Island. The
son of a prosperous chief, who owned sixty slaves, and traded
tobacco and salt for gold with the upland Hausas, Perault
had been captured in a battle with the Dorahs. When he
was sold to a Captain Delaware at Goree, a brother-in-law
had found him and offered to redeem him for three slaves.
But the kinsman needed time to go home to fetch the purchase price and the captain couldn't wait; no captain could,
and Perault went to South Carolina.

Perault brought with him not only his knowledge of African dialects but of French, a circumstance that gave him
interesting contacts with the "French company," made up
of slaves who had come up with their masters from San
Domingo. To this he quickly added English, and his master,
J. Strohecker, swore by him. When friends objected to Perault's "open, frank, and blunt manner" as unsuitable to a
slave, Strohecker retorted that the bluntness never had the
intention of giving offense, and that the man "would rather
suffer death than deviate from the truth."

From the mouth of the Oil Rivers, which even in the early
1800's no one associated with the great Niger, came many
Ibos, one of whom, Monday Gell, became even better known
than Perault. Gell not only learned to speak English fluently,
but somehow, though strictly speaking this was illegal, acquired equal fluency in reading and writing it as well. He
also learned the trade of harness maker, and became so
skilled that his master, John Gell, set him up in shop on
Meeting Street. Here, like many other slave artisans, he enjoyed almost as much independence as if he were free. He
drove bargains, kept accounts, collected what was due. His
relation with his master was more like landlord and tenant
than master and slave; he paid his master a yearly sum, the
amount the latter would have received from hiring him out,
and did as he pleased with the rest.

The surplus was apparently adequate for pleasant living.

An excellent workman, Monday Gell enjoyed the patronage
and respect of a fastidious clientele. His shop, centrally
located not far from the fine old churches of St. Michael's
and St. Philip's, became a rendezvous for Negro notables and
his own Ibo friends. By white and black alike he and his wife
were affectionately known as Pa and Ma Gell.

Perhaps the largest group came from south of the Equator,
from Angola. These "Gullahs" also produced a notable, Jack
Pritchard, better known as Gullah Jack, heir to a line of
Angola priests. What employment Paul Pritchard, his master,
put him to is not on record, aside from one reference to his
being at Pritchard's wharf. But Jack, slight in build, with
small hands and feet, would seem an improbable choice for
a longshoreman. He enjoyed considerable liberty of movement, and often visited plantations out of town, especially
Bulkley Farm, which had a Negro overseer.

Among the whites, Gullah Jack enjoyed no fame compar-
able to that of Perault or Monday Gell. Among his fellow
Angolas, and even among American-born members of African Church, which Jack attended, his fame was great. He was
what white folks called a conjurer, skilled in divining the
future and in casting spells. As such he was at the center of
the current African renaissance. His master heard something
of this source of prestige, but seeing no harm, was not moved
to investigate. He best knew Jack for his childlike pride in
a fine set of whiskers, which no persuasion could induce him
to shave, and for an equally childlike fondness for entertaining his white folks by playing the clown. Charleston families
still cherish anecdotes that go back to this period. There can
be no historical harm in attaching one of these to Gullah
Jack.

"Was you ever a cannibal?" young master would say.

"Course."

"Did you eat little children?"

"Plenty."

"What did they taste like?"

"Like pork. Only the fingers is better."

3.

Quite apart from the drama in which this period of "seasoning" was to culminate, the situation of the transplanted Africans living about Charleston in the decade and a half after the end of the slave trade is particularly interesting. Not only does it offer rare case histories, fragmentary but revealing, of Africans in transition—the "preconscious period" as some historians put it—but it gives a picture of a time and place where many Negroes, even as slaves, enjoyed unusual opportunities and privileges.

Superficially, many of them, especially the artisans and house servants living in Charleston, would seem to be more happily circumstanced than were many freedmen in the northern states. Absalom Jones and Richard Allen were currently gravely troubled by their parishioners' difficulties in maintaining themselves in a freedom so limited in economic opportunity as to seem often a cruel illusion. Could a beneficent providence have arranged for South Carolina to emerge from the Revolution committed like Pennsylvania to gradual emancipation, even supposing that the slave trade was continued as long as it was, its Negro population might have made the transition much more smoothly.

Given the promise of liberty, however far in the future, the Peraults, the Monday Gells, the Gullah Jacks would have had no incentive to engage in that admirably planned enterprise that was to give white Carolinians one of the scares of their history. But South Carolina had taken an irrevocable stand against adding to its population of free persons of color. Had not the troubles in Haiti started with this group? At the same time, almost perversely, thanks to the mellower trend of master and slave relationships that had come since Le Jau's time, many slaves were allowed a measure of quasi-freedom. It was a combination of circumstances that resulted in explosion.

South Carolina had long since outlived the crudities of its frontier days. Charleston was a lovely little town of fine houses and well-bred manners. There were assemblies where young girls could be presented to society; there were concerts, there was a race course where blooded horses could test each others' mettle. There were gardens and shade trees, some of the latter drooping gracefully with the ghostly beards of Spanish moss. Onshore winds were salted with the taste of kelp; offshore winds were scented in their seasons with the honey of the vivid little star-clusters in the jasmine vines, the sweetness of honeysuckle and mimosa, and the pale waterlily bloom in the magnolias.

In the high-ceiled houses, servants relished handling the delicate china, polishing the embossed silver, and rubbing to a fine glow the massive mahogany and rosewood furniture. Body servants, male and female, took pride in pressing out good broadcloths and filmy muslins; nurses were as proud of putting their charges into freshly starched pinafores as if these pale exotics were their own flesh and blood. They also gave a careful eye to the manners of their nurselings, and when occasion demanded would not hesitate to box an unheeding ear or spank a bottom.

There were good and faithful servants in Charleston then, the kind who would say, and mean it, "We belong to them and they belong to us." There was, for instance, one Devany Prioleau who served in the household of Colonel J. C. Prioleau. In the household of Governor Thomas Bennett there were Ned, Rolla, and Batteau, so well mannered, so utterly reliable, that when his excellency was afield he had no hesitation in trusting his womenfolks, including a pretty daughter of Rolla's age, to their care. Devany was as faithful as he looked. The Bennett servants concealed virile aspirations behind their façade of perfect manners.

Masters in general had forgotten the days when white folk shuddered from their Negroes as Prospero had shuddered from Caliban. No one dreamed of refusing to take communion at Holy Table if Negroes were received there; far from shrinking at the thought of meeting her slaves in heaven, a white mistress would not consider it heaven at all if she couldn't have her people with her. The present relationship was symbolized by the fact that among the well-bred the term "slave" was seldom heard. It was "my servants," or, more affectionately, "my people."

Now that the Negroes were close to outnumbering the whites, especially in the country, most of the latter had forgotten that there had ever been aversion to dark skins and "country marks." Leave that to the Northerners, an incomprehensible breed who managed to combine vociferous talk of abolition and "inalienable rights" on the theoretical level with an icy standoffishness on the practical. South Carolina visitors to the North were shocked to find that their servants were forbidden to ride in the same coach with their masters, and that skilled Negro artisans, who being free had gone North to make their fortunes, were forced into menial service by the refusals of white laborers to work with them.

In South Carolina the gentry were disinclined to accept theories like abolition; put on the defensive, most of them would stoutly stand on Biblical precedent, the mystic business of the mark of Cain, and Paul's much more explicit injunction to servants that they obey their masters. But the practice, at least among the more genial sort, was often more permissive than in the North. Their houseservants were usually privy to all family secrets; master and mistress commonly indulged them in a freedom of speech and criticism that they would not have accepted from their peers. In such households the tie between servants and master was so strong as to move one judge to characterize slavery as "one of the most intimate of human relationships."

Here and there, usually in isolated country places, one found an aging master or mistress, who having outlived all other kin, contentedly accepted the lot of being governed by their "people." One aged spinster, long beyond taking an interest in the making of a crop, suffered a visit from the sheriff who came to sell her slaves to pay her debts. The plight of the lone woman, deprived at one blow of all that gave life warmth and meaning, was as pitiable as that of her slaves.

Sometimes there was blood relationship. This circumstance is probably irrelevant to the drama in Charleston in 1822, in which all the Negro actors were thoroughbred Africans. But it is true that the standards of South Carolina in this period were not exclusively "lily white." There lived in Charleston in the early 1800's the daughter of an African princess and a British naval officer, a Mrs. Hardcastle. Brought to South Carolina as a child just before the American Revolution, she had been as gently bred as any daughter of South Carolina. If in the years preceding her death in 1817 she was not so widely received by good families, this neglect was due less to her color than her conduct. She had caused scandal by reputedly becoming the mistress of an Irish rector.

There were other families, according to one judge a largish number of them, of known Negro blood who enjoyed all the civic rights of the whites, were received into good society and even held seats in the legislature. Their rights to such privileges went unchallenged until they got involved in litigation and someone found it to his interest to challenge them on the grounds that a man of Negro blood could not testify in a case involving a white man. It then fell to the judges to pass upon their status. Until about a decade and a half before the Civil War the usual practice was to pronounce them white if they were respectable, if their community accepted them, and if in their persons "the badge of servitude,"

that is, negroid traits, had disappeared. Unlike other Southern states, South Carolina had no law specifying the degree
of white blood, usually fifteen-sixteenths, that would entitle
a man to white privileges. In these early days the lack of
such a law seems to have made for social mobility; later it
would have the opposite effect.

4.

Houseservants were in a minority. The bulk of the Africans were plantation field hands. These in the neighborhood
of Charleston produced mostly rice. Such laborers lacked the
houseservants' opportunities to observe white men's customs
at close range. They learned English more slowly and more
imperfectly and few of them learned to read. Their lot in
the fields was more rugged than most work in the Great
House. In the growing and reaping seasons they were kept
at hard physical labor from sunup to sundown, and if they
loitered over the task, they were more apt to incur a flogging
than were the house servants.

There were compensations however. Frederick Douglass,
who did both field- and housework, found as a young man
the vigorous work in the fields almost exhilarating after the
stuffy restrictions of the house. The laborers shouted and
sang at their work. It was indeed compulsory. "Make a noise
there!" the overseer would yell when one part of his force fell
silent. Not even the most alert overseer could be everywhere
at once. His only control of field hands out of sight was to
make sure that they didn't get out of earshot.

For the newly arrived African, once his limbs recovered
from the dropsies occasioned by the confinements of the long
voyage, the plantation was reassuringly like home. There
too, in Dahomey, in Benin, in Manding, labor in the fields
was communal, and the laborers sang as they worked. Fires
were built for comfort at the edge of the fields even in the
hottest weather, here as there.

Hours were long, but the field hands compensated by adopting a slower pace. Sometimes in Douglass's experience young hands raced each other to find out how quickly a row could be hoed. This they did only in the absence of overseer; no profit in letting the enemy know that a comfortable pace was capable of acceleration. On some plantations, however, "task work" was imposed, on completion of which the slaves could do what they pleased; such hands worked briskly.

At the end of the day and the week their time was usually their own. During planting or harvest they might be too tired to make use of it, but they were securer in their Sundays than the houseservants, whose duties were often doubled on that day. They could work their own plots, take a dugout into the river and try for catfish, or just sit about quarters cracking a yarn or starting a song. Their quarters lacked privacy and often the most rudimentary of comforts, but they could take what ease they could find there without being constantly under master's eye. The overseer was supposed to inspect, but he could be always at it.

On the plantations and in town the most interesting class of Negro laborer was the artisan. Masters of the larger plantations found it to their advantage to put some hands to the way of learning the trade of carpenter or blacksmith. On Bulkley Farm, Polydore Faber was blacksmith. His master had no idea that under the inspiration of Gullah Jack, Polydore was in his spare time learning how to beat ploughshares into swords, or at least into rude sabers and pike heads.

In Charleston so completely had such labor been taken over by the Africans that white labor was superfluous. Already the newer immigrants were coming to town, Germans, Swiss, Irish, hoping to set up in trade, but they went away sorrowful, for they rarely found an opening. A slave, Peter Poyas, was the best ship's carpenter in town. He was honest, industrious, and expert; his white clientele waited their turn for his services, and no German or Swiss journeyman could hope to compete.

Another notable carpenter equally esteemed by the whites was Denmark Vesey. He was one of the free artisans, and his industry had brought him a measure of wealth. At his home on Bull Street there was always a black woman at the washboard or ironing board, attending to his linen. It was a comfortable home and capacious enough to receive his many friends, slave and free, who often dropped in of an evening.

Carters, draymen, coachmen, hucksters were Negro. African stevedores unloaded the ships; the fishing fleet and vessels in the coastal trade were manned by Negro seamen and sometimes managed by Negro pilots. The latter would serve only on sloops plying the rivers and the inlets among the sea islands; no matter how trustworthy a slave, teaching him navigation was asking for trouble. But ordinary seamen sometimes traveled far, often to the West Indies, and occasionally to the Guinea coast. But few slaves were taken so far; the ease with which they could jump ship when they found a place to their liking had discouraged the practice.

During the Christmas season, the traditional time for hiring slave labor, many slave artisans went about on their own, interviewing prospective employers in search of a good job for the year to come. Their labors would earn them their keep and a wage. By agreement with their masters they would turn over a portion of the wage; the rest was their own, and so was their time when they were off duty. Some artisans hardly saw their masters, except to turn over what was due and report their general whereabouts. In effect they lived under a system of contract labor. It was, however, a legal anomaly, since by law no slave could make any kind of contract.

5.

Sundays and holidays, all but the Fourth of July—slaveholders felt an odd embarrassment about admitting their

people to Independence Day celebrations—were lively occasions in Charleston. Even field hands flocked to town then.
The rivers were full of the dugouts that they paddled to
town, singing as they came. Some of their craft, used during
the week to carry produce to market, rivaled the massive
African canoes. On a gala day an indulgent master might let
them borrow one of these so that the hands could go to town
in a body.

In town many went to church. In the fashionable churches
belonging to Buckra, St. Michael's, St. Philip's and their like,
there would be room only for the high-toned houseservants.
But country folk took pleasure in passing these elegant meetinghouses to see the gentry in their fine clothes step down
from their carriages, and to relish the mellow tone of the
bells. When they went to meeting it would be to African
Church, which had no less than three meeting places, one
in the Hampstead area, one in Anson Street, and one in Cow
Alley.

African Church was a fruit of the labors of that tireless
circuit rider, Bishop Francis Asbury. It was Methodist; at
least it was Methodist so far as it came under the control
of the Reverend Mr. Morris Brown, presently to be ordained
as one of the first Negro bishops. At the outlying congregations, where services were conducted by class leaders, its
denominational affiliation might be more questionable. Old
Bishop Asbury, who died in 1808, would have been startled
at the content of some of the devotions as conducted by class
leaders Denmark Vesey and Peter Poyas—for that matter,
so would Morris Brown. It seems to have been one objective
of the more active class leaders to keep their pastor from
any clear knowledge of what was going on in his own congregation.

No outsider ever knew the full story of what went on in
African Church in the years just before 1822. There was
singing, of course; the folk expression to be known as the
Negro spiritual was evolving in those days. White ministers

passing a building where Vesey was expounding from a favorite text may have felt a twinge of envy at the full throated congregational response. Just as well that they didn't catch the text. Someone did hear that some class leaders were feloniously using Sunday School to teach their people to read. This discovery caused the closing of one meetinghouse in 1821.

In general Buckra, as white men were called, a term brought in from Calabar, looked on the activities of the Africans benignly and without suspicion. The near panic that had followed the successful Negro revolt in San Domingo gradually subsided. By 1820 it was all but forgotten. Never had the field hands been more orderly, never had the relations of master and servant been more pleasant. No white man watching the Negroes taking the air in their Sunday finery felt a qualm of fear at their numbers. They were his homefolk; being afraid of them would be like fearing his own children. He took pleasure in the seemliness and gaiety of their Sunday dress. Catching sight of one of his own servants he might feel a kind of paternal pride in noting how well they looked. James Poyas's old coat, neatly turned and skillfully fitted became Peter Poyas better than it had become him. Peter's wife wore with dignity and grace a gown in which her mistress had often received her guests at Sunday dinner.

CHAPTER TWELVE

CHARLESTON
CARPENTER

IN 1781 when the American Revolution was nearly at an end and the revolution in France and San Domingo still unthought of, a Captain Vesey of Charleston ferried a shipload of 390 slaves from St. Thomas to Cape François, in what would soon become Haiti. Among the slaves was a lively manboy of about fourteen who became the pet of the captain and his officers. They let him ride cabin class, share the food from their table, and gave him a resounding name, Télèmarque.

The boy may or may not have been African-born; the fact that in later life he was accredited with knowledge of African languages and even some contacts with Africa itself suggests that he was. In any case, he had been in St. Thomas long enough to become seasoned and get over his awe of white men. He expanded in the playful kindness of the ship's officers and attached himself to the captain with the same sense of feudal loyalty that Venture Smith had attached himself to his own master.

At Cape François there was a ready market for a youth so personable and alert. Captain Vesey took the price offered and went his way, giving no further thought to young Télèmarque. He had not, however, done with him. On his next return he was astonished that the buyer wanted his money back, accusing Vesey of having sold him an epileptic. Since the sale had been made with a warranty of soundness, the captain had to refund the money and repossess the boy.

No traces of epilepsy had appeared before and none came after. Probably the fits were hysterical, a psychosomatic result of the abrupt transition from the spoiled pet of a ship to the lot of a common slave. The fits cost the lad the opportunity of playing a role in the Haitian revolution that would later interest him profoundly. He gladly returned to the service of Vesey and became his good and faithful servant. He accompanied his master in "voyages all over the world," whatever that may mean, until presently he settled in Charleston, where his classical name was corrupted to Denmark.

In 1800 he literally won his freedom. He was then in his early thirties and a man of multiple accomplishments. He spoke French and English, several African tongues, had learned to read and write, and had become a master carpenter. As such he belonged to the favored artisan class of slaves who were permitted to hire out their services. It would have been thus that Denmark Vesey had the means to invest in the Bay Street lottery. He won $1500 and used the money to purchase his freedom and set himself up in his own carpenter shop. His master had let him buy his freedom for $600, though the entire winnings would not have been too high a price for so valuable a property.

Such a stroke of fortune must have had deep significance for a man imbued with the African doctrine of fate. The fortune lay not only in the winnings, but the timing; a few months later, thanks to the new South Carolina law on emancipation, it would have been all but impossible for him to have bought his liberty at any price.

As his own man, Denmark Vesey became a conspicuous figure in Charleston, respected by both Negro and white. The former looked up to him as a class leader in the African Church, which he had helped found; the latter respected his sound and punctual workmanship, the industry by which he had accumulated substantial property, including a fine house on Bull Street, and his good manners. White people looking in at his shop or passing him on the street liked to stop and pass the time of day with him. He was knowledgeable and his opinions interesting; some were later to recall that they had gone so far as to discuss with him the merits of an institution so sacred as slavery.

What, men asked, could make such a man discontent with his lot? He came and went as he pleased; no one interfered with his property or meddled when he entertained in his house. What possessed him to do what Vesey was later proved to have done? What one thing did he lack?

Unfortunately Vesey was never like Vassa—part of whose career resembled his own—in a position to compose his memoirs; nor would he under whatever pressure consent to make a statement of any kind. One can only guess at his rationale from general circumstances and his known deeds.

One thing Vesey obviously lacked was citizenship. Even his property rights were not secure, as Vassa well knew, thanks to the law prohibiting a Negro from testifying against a white man. A freedman as well known and well liked as Vesey, and under the protection of a distinguished family, would probably have no real trouble; in any dispute involving price or payment he could find a white friend to come to his defense. But protection was not justice. And freely as the white men engaged him in discussion, Vesey, a boy no longer, knew the distinction between a true meeting of

minds and patronizing indulgence. White men gave him the
same latitude they gave their house servants, the license of a
court jester. Denmark Vesey had outgrown his jester days.

Another restriction was the law passed immediately after
he became free. What he had achieved he could not confer
on wife and child. The best he could hope for was to buy
them and hold them as his own; even this would not insure
their future, and he could not do this much unless their
owners were willing to cooperate.

For Vesey the problem was complicated by the fact that
he had, or had had, multiple wives, seven according to Monday Gell, and a corresponding quantity of children. As of
1821 he could not have been an active polygamist; Morris
Brown, pastor of African Church, as concerned for purity of
morals in his congregation as was his friend Bishop Allen
with the membership of the Free African Society, would not
have suffered such a man as class leader. Nor is there credi-
bility in a late newspaper report accrediting him with a
harem and saying that "to his numerous wives and children
he displayed the haughty and capricious cruelty of an Eastern bashaw." What wives he had were slaves; he could not
have made like a bashaw in sundry slave quarters without
its becoming known to the masters; and had they known he
would not have enjoyed their universal respect.

The evidence is that polygamy with him, as with some
white men, was consecutive. There is reference to the woman
Beck, in the service of Major Hamilton, as Vesey's "former
wife," and with whom he seems to have remained on friendly
terms. When disaster came he took refuge with another wife,
unidentified. There is a vague reference to a wife seen at his
Bull Street home, but the witness may have confused the
identity of the women who worked at his ironing board and
cooking pots.

Whatever the situation, Vesey was married and he had
children. Only one of the latter, Sandy Vesey, is on record,

though the witness was not positive of the relationship of the "fat black fellow whom I think was Denmark's son, as he looked very much like Denmark, had a full face." This youth could read; that much his father had been able to do for him, and even this was done illicitly. More he could not do while South Carolina remained in the hands of the white masters.

In his youth, while still under the spell of his loyalty to Captain Vesey, such circumstances may not have troubled him. Under the care of white protectors the future of his children would seem comfortable enough. But shortly after he became free, South Carolina masters began to buy into the new lands opened up by the Louisiana Purchase and to transport their slaves thither. If a loved wife and her children were so removed, it would explain much in the conduct of Vesey.

This movement coincided with the influx of immigrants fresh from Africa. As Vesey became acquainted with Perault, Monday Gell, Gullah Jack and all their kind, his memory of nearly forgotten traditions must have revived. He would recall the African distinction between foreign and domestic slaves and the safeguards that protected the latter. In America every slave was "foreign," though his ancestors might have come to the country long before those of his master.

He recalled the sacredness of the African family. Here, though indulgent masters often made a pretty ceremony of the wedding of favorite house servants, and had the event inscribed in the church register, the marriage was no marriage; for marriage is a contract and no slave could make a contract. There were situations, some of which may have come to Vesey's attention in his wander days, when a couple who had married in slavery were considered to be living in sin after emancipation because they had not gone through the formality of a second marriage. They themselves might never know, but their children would when they applied for their inheritance and found themselves disallowed as bastards.

By this reasoning the much married Vesey had never been married at all, and his children were all bastards. He had small chance to train or control them. In America there was no way of teaching them reverence for the spirits of the ancestral dead who in Africa guided and guarded every pious household. Their lot was worse here than the children of African foreign slaves, who in the second generation were often given the privileges of the domestic. Every slave child born on American soil was in the plight of an African war prisoner, torn from his people, without rights or protection.

Even the gentler Gustavus Vassa, who on his return to America and to slavery had for a time resigned himself to his lot, recognized slavery as a state of war. When Vesey looked from his own good fortune to the prospects for his womenfolk and children, this concept of slavery grew on him, and with it the corollary that war could be carried to the enemy camp as had been done in Haiti. When he assessed the relative numbers of white and black, when he looked on the uncowed spirit of the new lot of Africans, he became convinced that such a war, carefully planned and executed, would have a more than equal chance of success.

He had reached this point in his reasoning when he was offered a chance to return to Africa. The offer, which he refused, precipitated his decision. He would stay, as he put it, "to see what could be done for my people here."

2.

By 1819 Vesey was confiding in a few trusted friends, especially artisans like the ship's carpenter, Peter Poyas. Providentially at this time a national crisis arose that gave him new impetus, the uproar over the question as to whether Missouri was to be admitted to the union as a slave state or free.

Missouri was part of the vast territory ceded by the French. Emigrants from all quarters of the country, north and south, had been pouring into the new lands; territories had been organized, and by 1818 both Missouri and Alabama applied for statehood. There was no difficulty about admitting Alabama, whose geographical situation made it a natural part of the slave belt, but when Missouri, well to the north, also demanded admission as a slave state, the fat was in the fire. The abolition movement, which had been in abeyance in the North because most people supposed that slavery was already on the way out, was suddenly and belligerently resumed. The debates on Missouri raged in and out of Congress for more than two years.

The debates were echoed in South Carolina papers and conversations. House servants like Vesey's "former wife" Beck, serving dinner to her master, who happened to be the intendant or mayor of Charleston, kept her eyes downcast but her ears open to indignant comment on the latest northern Fourth of July celebration, in which resolutions were taken that not only the Africans in Missouri but in all America should be free. Vesey read the papers and what he read he discussed with his fellows and sometimes with white men. He may well have known the English merchant Purvis, who had taken an African-born woman as consort and was at this time as gravely troubled about the future of his sons as Vesey himself. He certainly knew Andrew Rhodes, a shopkeeper just outside Charleston, who was to get in trouble by giving forthright expression to his conviction that Negroes had the same rights as white men.

Vesey reported the gist of such discussions to the friends who gathered in his house. He was to be charged with telling them that the Federal government had set them free and that their South Carolina masters were keeping the knowledge from them.

If he did, it is quite possible that Vesey believed what he said. He was literate, he was intelligent, but he lacked the benefits of a liberal education. Phrases taken out of context could have made a profound and misleading impression. His travels "all over the world" could hardly have brought him to Missouri. He may not have known where it was, but he did know places like Philadelphia where the public had committed itself to emancipation, and he could have confused abortive amendments providing for emancipation in Missouri with laws applying to the country at large. He was in the same situation as much better educated men, who living under a closely censored dictatorship, snatch at such stray phrases as come to them from the free world and read into them extravagant significance.

There would be a parallel a few years later in Jamaica when the vigorous Parliamentary debate that preceded emancipation filtered through to the slaves. The literate read about it in the Kingston papers; the unlettered paid good money painfully earned by selling their produce in market to get it read to them. They also learned from the "walking Buckras," rootless white men, often discharged overseers, who roamed the island, putting up for a night or two in the slave quarters. (There were "walking Buckras" in South Carolina too.) House servants carefully followed the table talk of their masters, who often discussed current events as freely as if their servants had no better powers of comprehension than their dogs.

From all this Jamaica slaves gathered that the king had set them free and that their masters were resisting the royal command. When they in turn organized a rebellion they did so with a sense of loyalty to his majesty so real that they mistook British troops sent to quell them for friends and allies.

There were striking points of resemblance in the psychological situation of the slaves in South Carolina.

3.

In 1821 Vesey was in his fifties and his friends referred to him as "the old man." He was getting along in years after a lifetime of hard work, and white customers who marked his absence from his work bench did not begrudge him a holiday.

Vesey was not, however, on vacation. He was working on the first step of a bold plan that called for elaborate preparation. The military details of the campaign he projected he entrusted to Peter Poyas, who had both indomitable courage and an almost Caesarian grasp of strategy. But the military phase had to be preceded by intensive psychological warfare. This was Vesey's work before 1822; he may have begun it as much as four years earlier.

In these times even slaves had some freedom of movement. In off hours they could paddle their skiffs on the streams, and if sundown or foul weather overtook them at another plantation, they could put up for the night in the slave quarters without incurring reproach provided that they were back at their own by shell blow. On the travels of a free Negro of such good repute as Vesey there was almost no restriction. It is believed that his travels took him up to a hundred miles from Charleston.

The times were lax and easy compared to what would come later, but not altogether unsuspicious. During this period one branch of African Church was closed for the misdemeanor of teaching slaves to read. Vesey had to move with caution, especially when he got into distant parishes where he was unknown. He would keep to the byways, and if a white man came his way, he would make his manners, humbly stepping out of the road and pulling his forelock. If he were questioned, asked to produce papers, he would be prepared. Many of his white friends would have gladly written him an affidavit, but since it was important not to draw attention to the range of his travels, Vesey probably composed such documents himself. He would be fortified with pretexts for being afield: he was seeking a relative, or a shipmate of the voyage from Africa, a relationship for which Brazilians had coined the word "malunga." With his knowledge of African speech Vesey could make such a quest plausible.

Thanks to his position as class leader he could also pass himself as a Methodist circuit rider, and in fact this was nearly the case. Vesey must have known Bishop Francis Asbury in the latter's old age, when he tirelessly rode circuit through the whole South and found his most responsive communicants among the slaves of Charleston. Sometimes the bishop had brought a Negro preacher with him.

But there were perils in such an explanation. Asbury had known the South too well to send Negro circuit riders on their own; those whom he ordained to preach, like Richard Allen, were expected to function within their own parishes. Vesey probably never risked this story. Only when he had made himself at home on a strange plantation and he had assessed the circumstances would he preach. Finding himself among Methodists or Baptists he would deferentially join the worshippers and in the natural course of events rise to make his own confession of faith.

Getting acquainted with the plantation life was his object. He listened more than he spoke, learning local conditions of labor, the quality of food and housing, the character of overseer and master. When his new friends learned to trust him, he would hear of the runaways, some of them camping in nearby swamps, depending on their friends to bring them a share of their rations. He would learn what made them run, what was done to them when they were caught. He would know how often master went away and at what seasons; he even knew what master had in the way of firearms, and where he kept them. He picked up details of local history.

Whether he got up the Santee as far as Camden, he certainly heard of the slave insurrection that was to have taken place in 1816 had not its leaders been betrayed. He may well have talked with conspirators that the white men had not detected.

The information would come piecemeal. So quiet, so discreet was Vesey's manner, that his interlocutors would hardly be aware of being questioned, or that while they talked they were being sharply appraised. Vesey probably never left a plantation without an exact knowledge of who its natural leaders were, or without having formed shrewd estimates of who could be trusted in an emergency and who not.

Probably he divulged his Charleston connections only to picked men. To get an invitation to preach he need only draw his Bible from his pocket to verify a reference. The devout would not want to miss a chance to hear the Bible expounded by a man who could read it for himself.

Master and overseer either never heard of such "shouts," as they called such services, or had no objection. An overseer who had got religion at one of the camp meetings that were in this decade spreading from the Kentucky mountains to the coast might welcome them. Some scandalized their employers by identifying themselves with the Negroes at their worship, singing and shouting with as much abandon as they. Vesey would not relish their presence; any white man in his congregation, however young and impressionable, would inhibit his choice of text.

Bishop Asbury had learned that the only text for Negroes universally approved in the South was the one about the good and faithful servant. To his peers Vesey would modestly disclaim enough learning to preach to Buckra. He would recommend seeking salvation "in the wilderness" like the prophets of old. Only in the kind of meeting that the slaves called "hush harbor" could he expound his favorite theme, which was Moses.

White men had long ago learned to discourage a preacher of any race from discoursing to the slaves on Moses. Except for the necessity of calling the ten commandments to the attention of their servants, they would have been happy if the Bible could be revised to exclude the whole book of Exodus. Their people, ill-equipped to distinguish between historical record and divine parable, were likely to draw parallels from the Egyptian bondage and its outcome.

But Moses was a hard character to suppress. As Mungo Park had learned in Manding, even the Kaffirs who had never met a Christian often knew all about him, and many of them must have brought this knowledge to America. Afro-Americans who like Vesey could read the Bible for themselves felt lifted on wings like eagles when they read the full story, and they drew their conclusions from the white man's reluctance to discuss with them the very core of the Old Testament. Here in Holy Writ was record of another people, God's chosen, who had endured bondage; and because they were brave and had faith, God had permitted them to redeem themselves. Even after they had come into the Promised Land and had achieved power and glory they did not forget or deny that they had been slaves. To them their former condition was no memory of shame, but proof of the greatness of God.

What had been could be again. There were other bondsmen besides the Israelites, and other promised lands besides Canaan. The island known to Columbus as Hispaniola and to later generations as San Domingo was one. Carolina might well be another.

Such in substance was Vesey's theme. This was the gospel he preached when he was able to find a "hush harbor" and surround himself with people whom he could trust. When he went away his congregation would watch their chance to gather again to relive the drama that had lifted their hearts. The narrative would be carried by a leader, the man

or woman with the best memory, best presence, best voice;
the congregation would chant in response.

In time the essence of Vesey's sermon would become
stylized, like the structure of folk ballads, and get fittted to
an air, heard perhaps from the piano at the Great House, or
by those who sat at the periphery of a circle at camp meeting,
or outside the country meetinghouses to catch what they
could through the windows of the services within. The song
would be derived and yet their own. White folk who heard
snatches of such singing would recognize a vague familiarity
and smile at the Negro's inability to sing "correctly." They
were singing better than correctly—mangnificently. They
were creating, as all folk artists do, with natural variations
between singer and singer and occasion and occasion.

"When Israel was in Egypt's land," chanted the leader.
And the people responded low, "Let my people go."
"Oppressed so hard they could not stand."
"Let my people go."

Then leader and followers joined in a massive chorus, singing in unison, men and women an octave apart, and the
muttered responses became a shouted command.

"Go down, Moses, way down in Egypt's land,
Tell old Pharaoh, let my people go."

The hush harbor would have to be farther out in the wilderness than any considerable body could go unobserved,
if their voices, swelling in volume as the leader carried them
towards the climax, did not sometimes carry to the ears of
a white wayfarer.

"No more shall they in bondage toil.
Let my people go.
Let them come out with Egypt's spoil.
Let my people go!"

But if the white man caught something of the somber passion of the song, he was unlikely at a distance to make out
the words. There was nothing ominous in the slaves' choos-
ing to assemble in hush harbor. It was after all inhibiting for
them to practice their devotions within earshot of their white
folks, who found cause for mirth in the anachronisms of the
preaching and in their inability to carry a tune according to
the music books' scales and standards. Besides, their people
returned refreshed from such assemblies, with a positive
zest for work. The obscure preacher from Charleston had not
neglected the "servants, obey your masters" text. Relations
between servants and master had never been more friendly
than in these years when the former had faith that the means
had been given them to set a definite term to their labors.

CHAPTER THIRTEEN

THE CONQUEST OF CAROLINA

CHRISTMAS had long been the great jolly feast of the bondsmen wherever slavery existed in the Americas. Then, when they could best be spared from the fields, they were free, always for a day, sometimes for three, with indulgent masters for all the days until New Year's.

They were free not only of their labors but of many hedging restraints. The Africans got themselves up in tatters of costume suggesting the homeland, made themselves noisemakers of conch shells and anything they could beat with sticks, and in ragged military formation uproariously descended on the Great House, sometimes ousting their masters when they got there. At least that was what was sometimes done in Jamaica, where most "masters" were only overseers.

Around Charleston in Vesey's time, Christmas was less rowdy. But even here the slaves were allowed to roam, dance the night away on the threshing floor, and some masters broached a keg of whiskey for the occasion, though spirits were normally forbidden to their servants. Frederick Douglass, speaking of such festivities in Maryland, said that masters could hardly have controlled even the most docile of field gangs had they not given them something to look forward to.

When field hands came to the Great House shouting "Christmas gift! Christmas gift!" their folks were ready for them. Preparations had been going on for days to make up little sacks of candy and cakes for the children, portion out sides of bacon to supplement the rations for the grown folk, sort out new ribbons and mistresses' old gowns and masters' old coats to give to favorite house servants. It paid masters to be generous with what they were ready to discard. Otherwise, when they visited the dance that night they might find their newest and best circulating the floor on the persons of their most trusted servants. The latter would only laugh when caught, expecting master to appreciate a joke. This was their carnival, supervised by the Lord of Misrule.

Generous masters lent themselves wholeheartedly to the spirit of the thing. A mistress would lend a bondservant whose relation to her was almost that of a young sister her best ball gown, to have the pleasure of her pleasure and to insure that she cut a more brilliant figure than her rivals.

Country people thronged to Charleston as they did on Sunday to enjoy the sights and contacts, to parade in their best by the Battery and on Meeting Street. On Christmas 1821 an acute observer might have noted (though none did) that after a bit the crowds somewhat diminished. Inconspicuously, one by one, certain men withdrew from the gaudy parade to repair quietly to a house on Bull Street.

Vesey sat there to receive his general staff: Peter Poyas, who had long known his mind; Mingo Harth, three servants of Governor Bennett, Ned, Batteau and the eighteen-year-old Rolla; the Senegalese Perault; Gullah Jack. Monday Gell came too, but he could not yet be persuaded to abide. Alone of all this group, the carriage maker was nervous and uncertain. For now Denmark Vesey had ceased to speak darkly and in parables.

The subject of this conference was not the children of Israel; it was a daring plan for the future of Charleston. The events discussed were still months away, but the time had come to lay the groundwork of Poyas' grand strategy. Recruiting would begin at once, and each member of the staff would be procurement officer, forming a company of the people he knew best. Gullah Jack would recruit Gullahs; Perault, whose French was even more fluent than Vesey's, would help him form the "French company" from Negroes whose masters had taken them from San Domingo. It was troublesome that Gell still vacillated, for he was indispensable as recruiter of the Ibos.

The large artisan class, slave and free, was the province of Vesey and Poyas. One class was to be avoided, the house servants, or any who showed gratitude for presents "like old coats" from their masters. Poyas as chief of staff issued this injunction. "I will speak to them," he said.

A larger group was not to be enlisted at all, the women. What part they played would be inadvertent, like the information that Vesey picked up from the presence of Beck in the household of the intendant of Charleston. Making a more direct use of them would be dangerous; women who had the care of white children would counter Vesey's thorough ruthlessness with the treachery of pity. Besides, if plans miscarried, there must be some left free of dangerous knowledge to protect their own children. Vesey was well aware of the chance of betrayal now that his campaign was entering its critical stage, and from his knowledge of the incident at Camden he knew how it could happen. He imposed another security measure. Each officer would keep his own roster and keep it to himself. The central organization was

divided into autonomous cells, whose members, and to some
extent the leaders, would not know the identity of each
others' recruits beyond the contact man in the next company
and the courier assigned to maintain liaison.

2.

In his work as class leader Vesey now used texts that must
have surprised those who hardly knew that the Bible contained an Old Testament. He turned from the Beatitudes,
from injunctions to forgive the wrongdoer seventy times
seven, turned above all from the theme of "servants, obey
your masters," to the opening of Zechariah 14: "Behold a day
of the Lord cometh when their spoil shall be divided in the
midst of thee. For I will gather all nations against Jerusalem
to battle; and the city shall be taken and the houses rifled
and the women ravished." He turned to the bloody book of
Joshua and found in its protagonist an example and guide.
"And they utterly destroyed all that was in the city, both
men and women, both young and old, and ox and sheep and
ass, with the edge of the sword."

Like the Puritan theocrats of long ago, Vesey found a
direct personal application in such texts; in Charleston he
saw another Jericho, and in Poyas a man worthy to stand
beside Joshua.

But there were limits to the plain speaking he could carry
on within African Church. Too many, including the pastor,
had been infected with gentler versions of Christian doctrine. He had to keep his plan from the ears of Morris Brown.
He made his real exhortations before carefully selected
groups in his own house, and even so he ran into opposition.

"My God, what a sin!" one man exclaimed when Vesey
explained the necessity of putting not only the white men to
the sword but their women and children. "It's a great sin."

Vesey cited the book of Joshua, where the children of
Israel had slaughtered the entire population of Jericho ex-

cept for the family of the loyal whore, and this with Almighty God's express approval. He also cited military necessity from what he understood of the long struggle in San Domingo. Like the white men he saw it as purely a slave revolt; what he said was that on the island the Africans had been unable to get the upper hand until they steeled themselves to ruthlessness.

In casual meetings on street corners he mentioned the Congressional debates on Missouri and the conclusions he had drawn from them. After all, if the white men went to the lengths that they demonstrably did to keep the slaves from hearing of Moses and Joshua, would they not go farther to prevent their hearing that Congress had freed them?

With the literate he used classical precedent, recommending that they buy "the spelling book" and take to heart the fable of Hercules and the wagoner. Hercules had come across a wagoner who was praying to the gods to free his wagon from the mire. "You fool, stop praying and put your shoulder to the wheel," said Hercules.

Sometimes opposition roused him to flashes of a temper that was to be called "ungovernable and savage." There was his reply to a man who answered an argument on the unhappy lot of the slave with "But I'm living well."

"Others are not!" thundered Vesey. "Fools like you are in our way, and we shall mark you." He instructed his leaders to supplement their rolls of recruits with a smaller, more sinister list; on it were the names of slaves who for their folly must die with their masters.

Early in June, when all plans were matured and awaited only the signal, Poyas met the man to be known as Witness B, who spoke of a mission that the whites were setting up for the blacks. "See the good they are going to do us," he said.

"What of that?" asked Poyas. "Have you heard that on the Fourth of July the whites are going to create a false alarm of fire and every black that comes out will be killed in order to thin us?"

"Do you think they would be so barbarous?"

"I do," said Poyas. "I fear they have knowledge of an army from San Domingo, and they would be right to do it, to prevent us joining that army if it should march towards this land."

The excuse for the Fourth of July story was the mystery with which this day had become invested for Africans. They were excluded from the celebrations lest they get wind of the more debatable statements in Mr. Jefferson's Declaration. Slaves might well draw fantastic conclusions about so occult a ceremony, especially when it was observed to include bonfires and fireworks. That Poyas, whose hard-headed grasp of reality is demonstrated in the efficiency of his military preparations, believed his own story seems unlikely; but the moment was tense, and like Vesey he could fire up at opposition.

The reference to San Domingo had more sense in it. Monday Gell, who had finally overcome his scruples and joined the general staff, had written a letter to President Boyer of the Negro republic and had entrusted it for delivery to a Negro cook on a Yankee schooner. Boyer was at the height of his fame. He had just succeeded in ousting the Spanish, who had been occupying the eastern and most fertile end of San Domingo. Now that the whole island was under his control, the future of Haiti looked bright. But Boyer never answered the letter. Either he never got it, or with the Spanish threatening to resume the contest, he drew the line at taking on the forces of the white man's republic to the north.

Vesey seems to have sent some sort of appeal to mysterious contacts in Africa, perhaps in Sierra Leone. But neither was Africa disposed to undertake the conquest of the United States of America.

Some of the potential recruits protested not on moral but practical grounds. One thought that hands from the outlying plantations would be of little service if they brought with them no better weapons than their hoes, axes, and scythes. When Poyas sketched his plans for taking the Charleston Arsenal in order to arm them when they came, he was warned that such plans would be betrayed.

"My man, God has a hand in it," said Poyas earnestly. "We have been meeting four years now and have not yet been betrayed." He added coldly that he would know how to deal with informers.

The most picturesque recruiting was carried on by Gullah Jack, who acted as a kind of courier-evangelist to some of the nearer plantations. Poyas and Vesey, whose prevailing mental attitude seems to have been coldly rational, probably did not take seriously Jack's skill in conjure, or share the common view of him as "the little man who can't be shot or taken or killed." But in working among the African-born, especially the Gullahs, they could hardly have got along without him.

Jack was not without his practical side. While he was rousing his followers with mystical rites, he did not neglect to see that the blacksmith Polydore Faber added regularly to the cache of pikes and sabers on Bulkley Farm. Once he confessed to a confidant that there was one thing against which his magic was powerless, the treachery of "one of his own color." He was also practical enough to shave off his fine black whiskers, much to the surprise of his master, who knew how proud he was of them, when the day of action drew near, apparently to the end of making himself difficult to identify.

But he stood in the relation of high priest to his followers, and to them his powers were as awesome as those of Moses, who, it must not be forgotten, was among other things a very great medicine man. His influence was hypnotic; one man was to testify that he had no will of his own, hardly knew what he did until Gullah Jack's spells were broken. Once he arranged a symbolic feast at which he tore a fowl apart.

"Thus we will pull Buckra to pieces," he said. When the day of battle drew near, he distributed ground nuts and consecrated crab claws to his troops with directions for their use. "Eat nothing else on the morning when it breaks out, and when you join us as we pass, put in your mouth this crab claw and you can't be wounded."

By this time the day had been appointed. It was Sunday midnight, July 14.

3.

Circumstances both astronomical and social had governed the timing. The advantage of striking at midnight was self-evident. The advantage of the midnight chosen was that the running of the tides would hinder whites summering on the sea-islands from coming to the defense of the city and ease the progress of allies coming downstream from the parishes. Sunday was the day when countryfolk could flock to town without attracting attention. They would attend church, wander about in their usual harmless fashion until the time to return to their canoes, then, as would be expected of them, they would vanish. A few would paddle the dugouts home, where there would be later use for them, but most, having dropped in for a visit at the homes of friends, would quietly remain there.

In July most of the masters would have got their families away from Charleston during the malaria season. Malaria may have been one revenge of Africa upon America; it is possible that South Carolina mosquitoes, hardly less a nuisance than those of Guinea, were innocent of this contagion until they drank infected blood. Vesey was unwittingly aided by natural biological warfare. As the fever season approached, as the true Southern magnolia opened its aloof blooms among its glossy foliage, he could count on a general exodus of the more prosperous white folk.

Some of the wealthy would go north to Saratoga Springs,

or even to Europe. Others would move their families to the two places considered malaria-free, the sandy beaches of the sea-islands, or the pine barrens of the uplands. Advantage both military and moral would accrue from this. There would be fewer of the ruling class to interfere with Vesey's plans, and the unpleasant necessity of massacring entire families—there were still some who were squeamish about this detail—would be reduced to a minimum.

At the appointed midnight the uprising would occur in both town and country. On the plantations the slaves would kill their overseers and any owners in residence, seize what they had of arms and ammunition, and set out for town. Some would march overland; more would come down the Ashley and Cooper, which converge at Charleston, and some would come down the Santee. Many riverside plantations had huge barges for conveying produce for market, some capable of carrying as many as a hundred men; they would would be so used.

By the time they made town, Jericho would by God's will have fallen, and their services would be required only for mopping up operations. While they were overwhelming their masters in the outer parishes, the companies in town would not have been idle.

Here the plan was to attack from half a dozen different points simultaneously. Three of the immediate objectives were the Arsenal and the two ammunition depots. They must be taken at once, not only to prevent the white men from forestalling them, but to get arms. For some time Vesey had been levying his own company to get the means of buying guns and powder; but the levies, only 12½¢ a person could have brought him little more than enough to attack the guards.

Overwhelming the latter would not be difficult. They carried muskets, but the times were so trouble free that the muskets were not loaded. Vesey and Poyas may not have

known that, and spared no effort to effect this initial and
critical part of their strategy with deadly efficiency. They
themselves would conduct the attack on the Meeting Street
Arsenal, opposite St. Michael's. That the sentinel's suspicions
would not be aroused by the approach of black men at an
hour so long past curfew, both would whiten their faces and
wear wigs made for them by a local barber. While the golden
tones of St. Michael's bell still hovered in the air after the
sounding of midnight, they would have surprised the sentinel, killed him, and their followers, summoned from the
shadows, would be forcing the Arsenal doors. It was an operation that could be done without noise or the use of batter-
ing rams; there was only one door and it was of wood.

Other sentinels would be killed and the other depots
forced at the same moment. Ned Bennett was in charge of
seizing the one on the Neck, after which his task was to fire
the mills belonging to "old Buck," which was his off duty
name for His Excellency, the Governor of South Carolina.

Fires were to be set at several points, and as the whites
came out to give the alarm, they would be picked off. So
would any of their servants who offered opposition or were
known to be undependable. The companies of insurgents,
each under its own leader, would fan out from the depots
where they had taken their arms along appointed lines of
march until they controlled the city. The waterfront was a
primary objective. When the company assigned to this detail
had its arms, it would board the vessels lying at the wharves,
kill all their crews except blacks sworn to cooperate, and
capture the captains. Some of the latter must be preserved,
for if plans miscarried, they would need the vessels in order
to escape, and navigators capable of getting them to San
Domingo.

Yet how could their plans miscarry once they were put in
operation? When eventually the whites grasped the strategy,
their feelings included genuine admiration. They could not

conceive its failing, except for the one accident that did happen.

Given success, what then? Could Vesey have expected to hold tidewater South Carolina indefinitely and establish there a Negro state like that on San Domingo? Did his acquaintance with the hyperbole of Congressional debate lead him to believe that he would have Congressional approval of his *fait accompli?* Or on the basis of his appeal to President Boyer of Haiti did he believe that the American mainland could be conquered from the islands with his aid and the mysterious help that he seems to have expected from Africa? It is at this point that one most regrets that Denmark Vesey never wrote his memoirs.

The only account ever given of these plans, furnished by a Negro who did not admire Vesey, was that having looted the city, he planned to load the loot and his followers on vessels in the harbor and force their captains to carry them to Haiti. There was nothing visionary about this plan; it lacked the grand manner, but it could have been done.

However, Vesey's plot suffered the same fate as dozens of plots that were being hatched in contemporary Brazil. The slavers still plied between Africa and South America; African enclaves were being established throughout Bahia; regularly one of them planned a revolt against the whites, and as regularly they were betrayed. No matter what oaths were sworn on whose ancestors and whose gods, there was always one conspirator whose softness of heart impelled him to give a private warning to his own master. What happened so often in Brazil also befell Vesey in Charleston.

CHAPTER FOURTEEN

GOOD AND
FAITHFUL SERVANT

ONE FINE Saturday after-
noon in late May, Devany, a servant in the Prioleau household, went to market to buy some fish. While he went his
rounds, sniffing for freshness and prodding for firmness, he
became aware that a man whom he knew only as a servant in
the Paul household on Broad Street was taking an interest.
When Devany filled his basket and strolled to the wharf
below the market to take the air before going home, the man
followed him. They stood together a moment looking out at
the ships; then the man spoke.

"I've seen 76 before, never 96," he said.

He was speaking of a flag flying from a masthead. The
remark was a mere conversational opener, but because of
what came next it took in Devany's mind cabalistic significance. The stranger glanced quickly about him and then
spoke low: "Do you know that something serious is about to
take place?"

Devany did not. If Poyas, whose business it was to approach his kind had ever considered doing so, he had dismissed the thought. Good and faithful service stood out all over Devany. He stared blankly.

"Well there is," went on the stranger, "and many of us are determined to right ourselves. We are determined to shake off our bondage, and for this purpose we stand on a good foundation. Many have joined, and if you are willing to go with me, I will show you the man who has the list of names who will take yours down."

That at least was the gist of it. Somehow these words lack the flavor of old Charleston, but this is how they were recorded.

For Devany it was as if a thunderhead had darkened the bright afternoon. He was afraid of the sinister stranger. He looked down at his basket of fish and wished that he and it were safely home. But the stranger blocked his path, demanding an answer.

"I'm satisfied," said Devany at last. "I'm grateful to my master. I don't want a change."

The stranger melted away. He had made no threats; he hardly needed to. Devany stood like one paralyzed, stricken with terror and a queer sense of guilt. He had heard what he should not have heard; he was in the predicament of a child victim of rape who can confide in no one because the whole set of her training has taught her that what has been done is unspeakable. He dared not even go home. By chance a man whom he could trust came his way, Pensil, a free man of color. To him he whispered what had happened, and Pensil's reaction was forthright.

"Go home at once and tell your master," he said.

By ill fortune Colonel Prioleau was away and not due back for some time, but Devany dared not wait. He had been too stunned to ask the stranger for details; for all he knew the rising might be scheduled for that night. He sought his mistress and young master and stammered out his story.

He must have sounded rather comic, especially as he began as he always would with reference to the numerals, which now seemed to him to contain the whole key to the plot. Apparently Mrs. Prioleau and her son were amused and dismissed the story as they did the tall yarns of their people with the phrase "Negro news." Either that, or Mrs. Prioleau was the sort of wife who wouldn't call the fire department without her husband's express permission. She let the matter rest until her husband came home, and that was five days later.

When on May 30 the Colonel heard the story he did not take it lightly. Within the hour he was at Intendant Hamilton's office; two hours later, at five in the afternoon, the entire Corporation, what Charleston called its city council, had assembled with Governor Bennett to cross-examine the trembling Devany. The latter still knew his informant only as a member of the Paul household; the entire male staff was brought to the guardhouse, and from the lineup Devany picked William Paul.

He must have been a recent and imperfectly instructed recruit, else he would have known better to approach the likes of Devany. Curiously enough, he whose misdirected zeal was responsible for giving away the plot was, for want of evidence, never to be convicted. Now he denied his conversation with Devany and any knowledge of conspiracy. They locked him up for the night in what they called the "black hole" in the workhouse; by morning, when they talked of hanging, Paul was sufficiently demoralized to let slip two names. He suggested that Peter Poyas and Mingo Harth might know something of the affair.

At this point the Corporation was nearly ready to agree that Devany's story was "Negro news." If they had held a contest to pick the two Charleston slaves least likely to make trouble, they might well have come up with these. Though they arrested both on May 31, the necessity embarrassed them. The pair, gentlemen both, put them at their ease. They were at once solicitously concerned for the Corporation's anxiety and amused that they of all people should be held suspect. They welcomed a search of their quarters; if Poyas had, as was later charged, a list containing the names of 600 rebels, he knew better than to keep it where white men could find it. In Harth's quarters they found nothing at all, and in Poyas' only a letter, an odd document, containing the phrase, "Fear not, God that delivered Daniel is about to deliver us." It says much for the conviction conveyed by Poyas' manner that the magistrates dismissed it as irrelevant, and that even later, when they had a more comprehensive view of the man's activities, they found in it no cause to incriminate the writer, who was Abraham Poyas.

Harth and Poyas were released, and Devany and Paul held for further questioning. These must have been miserable times for Devany, who was now their only real suspect. But he would have sooner followed Daniel into the lions' den than venture into the streets of Charleston.

2.

Poyas was safe for the moment, but he and Vesey were faced with the necessity of changing their plans. They no longer dared wait until July 14 to strike. Now that the whites were suspicious there were too many chances for exposure. Free or not, Harth and Poyas would be watched. The white men would make it their business to know who came and went at their homes, and might call in members of their classes at African Church, many of whom were recruits, for questioning.

The arrest of William Paul had not passed unnoticed. Members of the movement who had wavered at first, like Monday Gell, might waver again under stress too prolonged. There was no knowing what else the prisoner might reveal under pressure. Already Paul had named two members of the conspiracy; eventually he might be forced to name people less superbly equipped than Poyas and Harth to keep their self-possession.

The conspirators kept their lines of communication open to watch for hints of further betrayal. It was not entirely for auld lang syne that Vesey had renewed acquaintance with his former wife Beck. It was unwise for him to visit her too frequently at the Intendant's house, and he didn't need to. He had her daughter-in-law Sarah cooking for him in his yard; Sarah could maintain liaison for him without even knowing she was doing it.

Rolla and Ned had an even better listening post in the house where they served, the home of Governor Bennett. At the end of the first week in June, William Paul, miserably afraid of hanging, let out other names, one of them Ned Bennett's. Ned heard of it at once, perhaps through his master, and took bold action. Without waiting to be summoned, he presented himself for examination. His open-browed candor impressed the Corporation tremendously. He was sent home.

Now on June 8 the uprising was little more than a week away, for Vesey and Poyas had decided that the best chance was the boldest. They had set the time a month ahead, to Sunday, June 16. So doing was difficult. It was hard enough under the circumstances to maintain contact with the nearer parishes; sending couriers to announce the change to the remoter districts was impossible. But their hands were strengthened by the fact that in spite of the cowardice of William Paul, the Corporation had extracted no information of real use to them. Acting quietly it had looked to the town's defenses, had increased the guard at the arms depots, had discovered and corrected the fact that the sentinels carried unloaded muskets. Beyond this they had accomplished nothing. The few people William Paul had been induced to accuse had given convincing accounts of themselves, and each had been defended by an indignant master.

Until almost the eve of rebellion they had nothing to go on. Not until Friday, June 14, did they get intelligence of real value.

By avoiding subjecting their followers to too long a strain, the leaders had had to take another risk. Some people who could contemplate violence calmly so long as it was at so safe a distance in the future as July felt differently when it faced them at close range. This seems to have been true of those members of African Church who had originally been in the white Methodist congregation. One of them, Billy Palmer, lived in the home of the Reverend Mr. Palmer, where he had been brought up from childhood as one of the family.

It was such people who, though pledged to rebellion, had protested indiscriminate slaughter. They wanted to spare not only women and children but ministers. One of these— was it Billy Palmer himself?—watched for an opportunity to give Palmer at least a chance to escape. The opportunity came on June 14 when the minister confided in "a trusted slave" that he had heard rumors of a rebellion in which Methodist slaves were implicated. It was then that the slave admitted that the rumor was true and that the uprising had been set for June 16. The minister went at once to the Intendant with this news.

It was now the turn of the Corporation to act with the coolness that Peter Poyas and Mingo Harth had shown. Since they knew so little, it was important to give the plotters an opportunity to betray themselves. To this end the authorities made no further arrests, though Palmer's informant seems to have done some name-dropping, and settled themselves to watchful waiting. The guards at the Arsenal had already been strengthened. They took one further precaution, the setting of armed patrols at every approach to Charleston. This they accomplished with such discretion that Vesey

knew nothing of it until after sunup on June 16 when his
courier, Jesse Blackwood, who had been sent on horseback
to carry intelligence to some of the plantations, returned
without accomplishing his mission. He had tried one road
after another only to find each way blocked by a possé of
white men.

Now Vesey knew that he had been betrayed, and by something worse than indiscretion. There was nothing to do but
wait. During the day small groups of country folk came to
him, paddling down the rivers, which seem to have been
imperfectly guarded. Vesey could only send them home
again with instructions to tell their companies to suspend
action until he sent word. The night of June 16, when Jericho
was to have fallen and its people slaughtered and spoiled,
passed without incident. The golden tones of St. Michael's
sounded midnight and nothing happened.

Next day the arrests began. All the manservants of Governor Bennett were taken, not only Rolla and Ned, but Batteau and Mathias. Peter Poyas went back to the guardhouse,
and with him James Poyas, four slaves belonging to T. R.
Smith, and Mrs. Lining's Amherst. Mrs. Lining wept when
her servant was taken, and indeed the magistrates could find
no evidence against him except that he had asked a class
leader to pray for him on the night of June 16. Having heard
some rumor of an "earthquake," a term used to refer to what
Vesey proposed, he had feared that the innocent would suffer
with the guilty. The court, which was sworn on June 19,
believed his story, and Mrs. Lining wept with happiness
when Amherst came safely home.

3.

When the trial began, an accusation was made that struck
the magistrates as preposterous: Denmark Vesey was said to
have masterminded the plot. They would not credit so arrant
a piece of "Negro news," inspired no doubt by envy. It was

not only that they liked Vesey; they had liked Poyas just as much and now had a whole dossier of evidence against him. It was the impossibility of imagining a motive. What could impel a freedman who had done so conspicuously well for himself to join a shabby conspiracy of slaves?

Negroes, as they well knew, had as keen a sense of class distinction as white men. House servants held themselves above field servants, artisans above both; mulattoes considered themselves superior to full bloods, and prosperous freedmen were a race apart. Vesey was none of your vagrants who lurked about the slave yards in hope of a handout. He had more property than many white men, everything to lose by anarchy and nothing to gain. They refused to make themselves ridiculous by arresting such a man.

Nevertheless, on June 22, when the evidence against him had accumulated disturbingly, they set out to find him.

At first glance the house on Bull Street looked reassuringly familiar; it bore no evidence of flight or panic. Women bent over the washtubs; Sarah stirred soup in the big pot in the yard. They looked up at the approach of the white men and said that Vesey had been called away. Where? They shook their heads in surprise; no servant asks master, black or white, his business. They knew no more than the magistrates.

They knew no more; but they undoubtedly knew as much. The trials were being conducted with extreme discretion. No newspaper had printed a word about them; no Negro was permitted to approach the courthouse except as called to give testimony; the courthouse steps, favorite lounge of the idle, had been cleared. At table, masters had been schooling themselves not to discuss current events before their servants. Nevertheless the latter knew everything they did.

It was easy to linger at the door after removing a course to catch the resumption of a conversation. It was possible to listen at the door of the bed chamber, especially as there were mistresses who required a womanservant to spread her pallet in the hall outside. Houseservants were in a peerless position for espionage, and not every servant was a Devany. The women had been insulated from dangerous knowledge, but what white folk knew they knew. Vesey, who was indeed in flight, had very likely acted on information picked up by Beck and relayed to him by Sarah.

They ran him down in the quarters of his current wife. A day later and they would have missed him; Vesey had arranged passage on a ship due to leave Charleston June 23.

In court they got nothing out of him. He listened to the charges with stony face and folded arms. When the testimony had been given, he cross-examined the witnesses with a ferocity that gave the white men their first inkling of a temper "savage and ungovernable."

Once he was surprised into an admission. He had denied planning to disguise himself as a white man in order to approach the sentinel. But when a wig made for him was produced in court, he was caught off guard. "Good God!" he said, and then admitted that it was his.

On June 27 he was sentenced to hang. The judges thought they saw tears in his eyes, and wished that they could interview him alone. To do so they would have had to remove him from the guardhouse, and that they dared not risk.

The multiplicity of prisoners had long since overtaxed both workhouse and guardhouse, which had not been designed for mass arrests, and prisoners could not be kept apart. Peter Poyas, for whose spirit they felt an almost chivalric respect, was under these conditions managing to control prisoners who showed signs of weakness. "Die like a man!" he said to a younger man, and the youth, meeting his eye, drew back from the brink of confession. "Die in silence as you shall see me die," he said again, and again he was obeyed. If the tears in Vesey's eyes betokened weakness, Poyas knew how to give him strength.

Poyas had revealed nothing. The case against him was

based on testimony from men whose identity the judges protected by code numbers and letters. From them they heard that there had been 600 enrolled in Poyas' company, but they never elicited so much as one name. In court Poyas' one interest was in learning how the plan had been betrayed. When a magistrate asked him if he would actually have participated in the slaughter of white folk, children and all, his only answer was a smile. It was such a smile as haunted those who saw it for years after. When he was condemned to hang he said only, and not as one who pleads, "I suppose you'll let me see my family first."

Jesse Blackwood, the courier, and the Bennett servants were condemned with him. Young Rolla Bennett, exhorted by a minister, gave some sign of repentance. When the Bible was read to him he said that if that psalm had been called to his attention before he would not have conspired against so kind a master as his.

It was a confession of sorts, but even Rolla did not turn informer. In town they were saying that the handsome youth had planned to make the Governor's sixteen-year-old daughter his consort. The source of this story was probably the testimony of the witness who said Rolla had told him that when the men were killed "we shall know what to do with the women."

He and five others, Vesey, Poyas, Blackwood, Ned and Batteau Bennett were condemned to hang on July 2. On the last day of June, Gullah Jack circulated the Bulkley farm crying in effect, "They shall not die!"

4.

Though the magistrates now had most of the ringleaders in custody, they still had no notion of the extraordinary diffusion of the plot, how far it had spread in the country outside Charleston. Gullah Jack was still at large. His master's surprise that "the little man with the big beard" had recently cut off the beard had not included suspicion. Surely a man may shave.

Gullah Jack was to have commanded one of the columns appointed to take the city, and his company was still intact. He now planned to set it on the march after midnight on July 1, overwhelm the guards, release the condemned, and carry out the original plans. To this end he whipped up the spirit of his followers.

But brute circumstance had impaired his hypnotic power. To his battle cry his men responded with the prudence of cowards: the city was too vigilantly patrolled and they too few to effect a rescue, let alone take Charleston.

"Coward! Give me back my corn and cullah!" cried Jack, the cullah being the consecrated crab claw. It was then he recognized that his magic would not work against black man's treachery. His name, it happened, had already come up in court; that he had not been taken was apparently due to his master's protest. There was pathos in the response of many masters to an accusation against a favorite servant. "But not one of my people! They worship the ground I walk on. I'd stake my life on it." Just so had Governor Bennett felt about his manservants, who nevertheless were hanged on July 2.

The execution was not segregated. Negroes were encouraged to look on. A fifty-year-old peddler, the German Jacob Dander, watched with them and suddenly turned on them. Vehemently in his broken English he denounced their cowardice for not defending their leaders.

He was reported; he was given opportunity to expound his views in court. Already the judges had heard something of a mysterious "white leader" appointed to give the signal for the rising. It might have been a reference to Vesey's disguise, but the judges were on the lookout for a white accomplice. They arrested Dander and eventually three like-minded white men, all in their middle years, all but one outlanders and transients.

Scottish William Allen had allegedly offered the insurgents his services, saying that "though he had a white face he was a Negro at heart." A Spanish sailor, whose name the magisterates rendered as John Igneshios, had said that he "disliked everything in Charleston but the Negroes and sailors." Andrew Rhodes, the local man who had a shop near town, said that the Negroes had as much right to fight for their liberty as any white people. All these faced court and got off with fines and prison sentences. The heaviest penalty, one year and $1,000 was imposed on the Scot, who did not deny his offer of aid, but claimed that a free Negro had first made him drunk on brandy and then offered him money.

The white men were not tried until the reopening of the trials later in the month. On the eve of the first hangings, the magistrates were ready to rest the case. There was a lull, during which Gullah Jack, now aided by Charles Drayton, continued to work among the field hands of the outlying plantations. Between them they mustered enough followers to set a new date for the uprising, July 6.

They too were betrayed, and by of all people the blunt-spoken Perault. Why this man became a turncoat is not on record. Possibly his master, knowing that he "would rather suffer death than deviate from the truth" had asked him a direct question. Perault first admitted his own complicity, and then under pressure implicated Tom, the black overseer of Bulkley Farm. Investigation of the farm brought forward the man known as Witness 10, and it was he who accused Gullah Jack.

Brought before court, the Angola, who knew that white men best liked black men when the latter showed themselves as great children, at first played the clown. His master had no evidence more incriminating to offer than his surprise at Jack's shaving his beard, and the accused played the fool so well that the magistrates were nearly exasperated into believing that he lacked the sense to lead anyone at all.

They turned to Witness 10, apparently a member of the Gullah Company, and when Jack heard what he and his kind had to say, he lashed out at his betrayers, and the court saw him in a new light as "artful, cruel, bloody . . . in short diabolical." They sentenced him to hang.

From then until the execution on July 12 Jack's conduct seemed to them contemptible. He didn't want to die; he pleaded for a reprieve. A man may be excused from wanting to postpone his own hanging; moreover, Gullah Jack still believed that the rebellion would yet take place, and retained stubborn faith in his priestly ritual. The cruelest thing the judges had done him was the ridicule with which they had accompanied his sentence. They had scorned his attempts to enlist "all the powers of darkness . . . the most disgusting mummery and superstition" and taunted him with the failure of his "boasted charms" to protect him. "The airy specters conjured by you have been chased away by the superior light of truth, and you are exposed, the miserable and deluded victim of offended justice."

Being spoken to thus before his betrayers was unbearable. Worse was the thought that it might be true, that God Himself was white. In the guardhouse Gullah Jack must have sought an inward privacy, no other kind being available, to sort out his thoughts, recall his strongest incantations, and pray to his priestly ancestors and all the gods of the African pantheon. It was unthinkable that these could not prevail against the white man's contumely. But Africa being far, he needed time to reach them.

The white men looked on in contempt when the conjurer went to the scaffold, not stoically as Peter Poyas had gone, but dazed and shaken. In giving him low marks for courage, they forgot one detail; demoralized though he was, he obeyed Poyas's command to die in silence. The blood of his men in the Gullah Company would not be on his head.

5.

While Gullah Jack was still trying to stave off the inevitable, two other ringleaders were arrested, Charles Drayton and Monday Gell. From these came sensational revelation; for the first time the judges learned the almost state-wide extent of the plot.

Recruiting Gell had been a mistake. Slave though he was, he felt no ignominy in his condition. He was nearly as much in charge of the prosperous carriage shop on Meeting Street as if he owned it, proud of his master's confidence in him and of the gentry's admiration of his workmanship. He had been given the supreme privilege of learning to read and write, perhaps in order to keep his master's accounts. A devout member of African Church, his independent readings in his Bible had impressed him more than Vesey with the charge "love thy enemies."

Vesey should have let him alone. But Gell had been persuaded in February to join the general staff, which, thanks to his fine round hand, made him its chief scribe. He had also set about recruiting his own Ibo company. Starting late he enrolled only forty; this was well, for when authority took him, he surrendered every name on his roster.

He did not do so at once. Like Poyas and Vesey he stood mute at his trial; it was only after the sentence of death that he yielded to a conviction of sin. There was now no Poyas in the guardhouse to still his misgivings. On July 13, the day after the death of Gullah Jack, he confided to Drayton his dread of dying with such guilt on his conscience. Drayton, who had already made a partial confession, reported Gell's state of mind to the Intendant.

To the latter Gell told all he knew; his followers, arrested in turn, made their own revelations. For the first time the authorities learned how much of the state, all the Tidewater region and areas far beyond, had been honeycombed with sedition. Thanks to the autonomy of each rebel company, they never learned everything. South Carolina slaveholders would wonder to the end of their days which of their people had vowed to cut their throats and might still if it could be managed.

It was no time for mercy. On July 22 there was a mass execution of twenty-two "on the line" of the old fortifications now marked by Line Street. Let those whose guilt was still undisclosed look on and repent.

Even then the case was not closed; on August 2 another ringleader, William Garner, was brought in from Columbia. But his hanging on August 9 was the end.

A slave insurrection was on a par with a ship's mutiny, a moral "earthquake" productive of unreasoning terror. It is remarkable that the magistrates had nevertheless acted reasonably and by their rights justly. They had made 131 arrests; of these they had released 59 as not guilty, and had condemned not to death but transportation 37 in whose conduct they had found extenuating circumstances. These included men against whom the evidence was inconclusive, like William Paul, and those who had turned state's evidence, like Perault and Monday Gell. Confession had not been induced by such promises; the confessors had confessed only to save their souls. Not until the case was disposed of were they told that their punishment would be exile.

There were also rewards. For all the cry that arose immediately that the state must be rid of the anomalous and dangerous class of free Negroes, one more member was added to this group, the good and faithful Devany Prioleau. A special act of legislature was passed for this purpose. Pensil was rewarded with $1,000 for his advice to Devany, and the latter given capital to set up in business as a drayman. After the notable hangings of July 22, the man finally dared venture on the streets again. Some of his people might remain aloof, refuse to admire his new glory as he sat in his own cart driving his own horse, but his white folk, a phrase which now embraced all the Charleston gentry, would never forget his claim on their gratitude. Devany was still driving his horse and wagon on the eve of what was to be known locally as the Confederate War.

CHAPTER FIFTEEN

THE WAY
OF BLOOD

THE Corporation of Charleston was proud of the expedition with which it had averted rebellion. Since newspaper stories had not been permitted while the suspense lasted, beyond a brief report of the hangings, it made its own accounting to the public in a pamphlet that went so far in candor as to acknowledge that the plot would almost certainly have succeeded but for its timely exposure. Later two citizens expanded the story to include in full the depositions of Witness 10, Witness B and their kind.

Both pamphlets were admirable in their objectivity and presentation of circumstantial detail. Then suddenly the sale was stopped; possessors of the documents were asked to destroy them. Reading the story, Charleston people for the first time felt something like panic. Vesey's plot had been too near a thing. If Poyas' roster had really included 600 names, the arrests had barely scratched the surface. It was madness to permit a blueprint for rebellion to lie about where slaves could see it.

Theoretically no slave could read. Yet the trials had disclosed a startling degree of erudition: slaves who pored over Biblical texts; slaves who went to the "speller" to see what Vesey had meant about Hercules and the wagoner. No use putting them to a literacy test, for they were experts in dissimulation. A book burning was the only solution. Soon after publication the pamphlets became the rarest of documents.

According to Monday Gell, women had had no part in the plot. But sometimes masters caught snatches of what the women crooned in their quarters and wondered.

"They crucified my Lord," one woman said huskily.

Others murmured a response, "And he never said a mumbling word. Not a word. Not a word."

It was their Good Friday song. But why sing it out of season? And were they really singing of the Lord Jesus, who on the cross had uttered seven last words? If Mrs. Peter Poyas or the nameless wife who had hidden Vesey for five days or even Beck murmured this song of mourning, of whom were they thinking?

Ma Gell could not lend her voice to theirs. Mutely she mourned her husband's transportation to Alabama; he had mumbled many words.

The women could lament only in their quarters. Their natural wailing wall, African Church, had been razed to the ground, and most of the congregation was still under suspicion. Their pastor Morris Brown had returned from Philadelphia on the ominously significant date of June 16 to find himself without a flock. He too had been arrested, for one witness claimed that he had given tacit approval to Vesey's plans. But the judges accepted Gell's statement that every precaution had been taken to keep him in ignorance. The Intendant kept him in protective custody in his own household until he felt that there was no danger of mob violence. Presently Brown drifted back to Philadelphia, where he would one day succeed Allen as bishop.

African Church was no more; white patrols had been set up to insure that the Negroes not gather in private places of worship. There was even a sentiment that Negroes should not be allowed any religious instruction at all. The Baptist minister, Richard Furman, opposed such counsel, holding that what the Negroes needed was not less religious training but more. He recommended the Pauline utterances in the book of Philemon where "a luminous exhibition is given of slaves and their masters enjoying membership together in the Christian church [and where] their respective duties are taught explicitly."

Nor did Dr. Palmer close his Methodist Church to the Negro faithful. They might come if they walked humbly and wore seemly dress; any sign of mourning, black bands for the men, black veiling for the women, not only debarred them from worship but exposed them to arrest.

As for the bereaved women of Charleston, own sisters to the Trojan women, who could pray and weep where Buckra were? Only in the kitchens, in their quarters, could they murmur what lay on their hearts: "They crucified my Lord. And he never spoke a mumbling word. Not a word."

2.

The discovery that a slave insurrection had its inception in the mind of a prosperous, honored, free man of color had a profound effect on South Carolina slave owners. Belatedly they looked into the motives that could inspire such men as Vesey to rebel. "They have sufficient liberty to appreciate the blessings of freedom, and are sufficiently shackled to be sensible that they enjoy comparatively few of these blessings."

The insight did not cause the slave owners to multiply the blessings so that no future Vesey would have an incentive for revolt. The remedy that a group of citizens proposed in a petition to the South Carolina legislature was that the entire class of freedmen be transported out of the state. They advocated a massive freedom ride in reverse.

Their petition was well reasoned, forcefully expressed, and refreshingly free of the usual cant about the divine authorization of slavery as found in the Bible. The authors were not addressing an abolition society, but men who like them accepted the institution as one of the ineluctable facts of life and were interested only in making it work.

They anticipated Lincoln's "house divided" philosophy in the sense that they demonstrated the impossibility of allowing free Negroes to live side by side with the slaves. Association with freedmen caused discontent among the latter, and a desire for liberty that the slave "can never hope to acquire by purchase or faithful service." They adduced the natural community of interest between freedmen and slaves, usually based on blood relationship, that had led them to cooperate on insurrection. Safety lay in extinguishing the very thought of freedom by banishing the freedmen "that we may proceed to govern [the slaves] by the only principle that can maintain slavery, the 'principle of fear.'"

Legislation so radical was never passed. Just as masters had stoutly defended slaves accused of conspiracy, white acquaintances would defend free Negroes threatened with exile. There had been striking examples in Virginia in 1803 after the passage of the law requiring every Negro to leave the state within a year of emancipation; the House of Burgesses had been deluged with petitions from white men asking that a Negro cooper, carpenter, laundress, baker be permitted to remain where he was because of his indispensable service to the community. South Carolina would have been hamstrung without its Negro artisans, who, slave or free, had a virtual monopoly of the trades. Nor could South Carolina forget that if one freedman had initiated the conspiracy, another, Pensil, had been instrumental in its disclosure.

The remedy was not to expel but to curb. Hereafter emancipation would be possible only by specific legislative act, and the activities of freedmen were to be so restricted as to make it impossible for a future Vesey to organize followers. There had always been slave codes; now most of their provisions were extended to the freedmen.

Hereafter no Negro, slave or free, could leave his own area without a pass, issued to the slave by his master, to the freedman by his legally appointed guardian. Like a military travel order, it had to be dated, signed and contain explicit information about destination and time of return.

Besides patrols set up to enforce this law, every white man became an enforcing officer. When he met a Negro wayfarer it was his duty to stop him, question his purpose, and examine his pass.

Assembly of any kind was forbidden. Negroes could not even come together for worship unless a white man of the appropriate denomination was present. It was the business of the patrols ("patty rollers" as the Negroes disrespectfully called them) to make regular rounds of the slave quarters to insure that under a lenient master slaves were not getting together to discuss the subversive activities of Moses.

Older rules remained in force. The free Negro had long been subject to taxation without representation, not only on his property but in a poll tax; if he defaulted he could be sent to the workhouse to work it off. It remained impossible for a Negro to testify in court against a white man. This law was universal in the slave states, though some judges in Louisiana and Delaware recognized that if Negro evidence was wholly disregarded "wrongs may be committed with impunity."

Such codes were not unlike martial law, especially in South Carolina where it had seemed as if a far more humane condition might be in process of evolution. Rule by "the principle of fear" imposed something like a state of war. So long as patrols were vigilant, it would be a cold war. A hotter war was in the making. When did the "Confederate War" become inevitable? Was it the adoption of the black code, or even earlier, in 1800 when it was made impossible for a slave to hope for freedom? Two men who would have something to contribute to the shooting war were born in that year when Vesey became a freedman, Nat Turner and John Brown.

The code was nearly as much a nuisance to white men as to black. This was especially true of the patrols. In the first fright after the Vesey affair, citizens in good standing so served; then as the excitement subsided and the duties became onerous, they relegated the responsibility to hired substitutes, mostly landless "poor whites," who being as much victimized by slavery as the Negroes, hated the slaves. A rough lot, seldom deterred by any sense of *noblesse oblige,* some of them committed abuses. There were court cases after they made off with hogs that masters had allowed their field hands to raise, or broke up a Christmas dance and tried to arraign the master for letting his family attend it.

Slaves were not after the first shock wholly cowed by the "patty rollers," whose movements could be anticipated, and with skill evaded. Illegal assemblies still took place in "hush harbor." Passes were forged. And even after the hangings in Charleston, former members of the notorious African Church showed as much spirit as the Free African Society of Philadelphia when white Methodists undertook to segregate them. Eventually they again had a church of their own.

If any conspiracy evolved in either African Church or hush harbor, it did not lead to revolt. It was not entirely a matter of the vigilance of the patrols; it was that without the periodic arrival of Africans imbued in the warrior tradition, the last vestiges of African tradition were being extinguished. There was nothing to remind the slaves that their fathers had been born free. Sometimes a slave turned with violence on a master or overseer; sometimes he took flight. These were individual incidents. Not again in South Carolina did any attempt the bold plan of wresting the land from the white men.

In Virginia there was an exception, and that most bloody. It was also true that in the northern tier of the slave states the spirit of Vesey and Poyas survived in the organization of flights to freedom seldom possible in a spot that lay so far under the North Star as South Carolina. The revolt was the work of Nat Turner; the most intrepid organizer of flights was the woman, Sojourner Truth. The one had been reared by an African-born grandmother whose mystic prophecies conditioned his manhood; the latter, as ignorant of her ancestry as she was of her letters, was nearly as African as if she had been born on the banks of the Niger.

3.

Sojourner Truth, born to slavery in New York some decades before emancipation went into effect, was a woman of towering stature and indomitable force of character. In her prayers to the God of the Christians she took an imperious tone. Was it due to the influence of her barely remembered parents that she performed her devotions beside a running stream, like an initiate of an African river cult? For her, prayer was what it had been for Gullah Jack, the driving of a bargain with God, a promise of return for value received. She was not, however, so African as to sacrifice cockerels and she-goats. As a member of a nominally Christian household she offered guarantees of good conduct. In her slave days this was the more difficult sacrifice. She was then living in what white folk called sin; she was mistress to her master. It bothered her that she couldn't always achieve the degree of virtue she had promised.

This did not prevent her becoming wroth when God in His turn failed to honor an agreement. In her riverside prayers she addressed Him with familiarity, sometimes in tones of command. It was the way she talked to her white folks and to white authority when the last of her sons had been taken from her and sold South just before New York law would have made him free. By sheer force of character she managed to get him returned. She showed similar force in her early dealings with God, treating Him much as an African priest treats the minor deities whose good offices are invoked in casting spells.

Then came to her the moment of revelation characteristic in the lives of the saints. One day she knew that God was not by the riverside only; He was everywhere; He could not be pinioned into the here and now, for He inhabited all the world and all eternity.

"Oh God," whispered Sojourner. "I didn't know you was so big."

She cowered before Him, and longed now for an intercessor, a friend to mediate between her and a Being vast as the sky. This too was African. Mungo Park had found that Kaffirs believed in the great God, but thought Him too remote to take an interest in their trivial affairs. Only the lesser gods and the ancestral spirits would listen; these they sought, perhaps less as a substitute for God than as an approach to Him. Africans who migrated to Catholic countries found their approach through the saints.

Penetrating her distress Sojourner Truth felt the presence of a spirit of warm lovingkindness and knew that the intercessor stood at her side. But who? In the tradition of the cult of the dead she named friends who had gone into the world of spirits. But in none of them had she known the radiant goodness that she recognized here. At last she whispered the name of Jesus and was at peace. It was Jesus who had come to help.

She had heard the name in the household where she served, as she had heard of Washington and Lafayette. She had classed these names together as names of eminent people, but of no significance to a poor serving woman. But now when she spoke this name she felt the lovingkindness enfold her.

From that day she who had begun life as Isabella, the sinner, evolved into Sojourner Truth, the saint. She never learned to read the Bible; she had it read to her preferably by children, for such would not interfere with the quest for the truth that lay within her by stopping for irrelevant interpolation. All her life became a searching in the body and in the spirit; and the spirit was pure, unclouded by dogma.

When she became free she entered her life work, guided by her intercessor. It was heroic work. Her towering gaunt figure had high and unmistakable visibility; yet again and again she invaded the border states to lead bondsmen to freedom. Thanks to her courage, her ingenuity, and above all her faith, she brought whole families through the devious stages of the underground railroad without once being taken.

4.

This piecemeal way of getting freedom did not appeal to Nat Turner of Southampton County, Virginia. He took Vesey's way, and like Vesey he had African inspiration. It came from his African-born grandmother, who had restrained his mother from strangling him at birth by pointing out marks on the baby's head and breast which signified that he was "intended for some great purpose." Like Gullah Jack she may have been of a priestly cult; just such marks enable the priests of Tibet to recognize the Dalai Lama among babies born at the appropriate season.

Like a dark goddess she hovered over his childhood, and was not surprised when he evinced miraculous gifts, such as relating events that had taken place before he was born, or spelling out the first book placed in his hands. There were probably natural explanations for both miracles; his white folks said that he had learned his letters from a young master. But his prowess was wonderful enough, and as a grown man Turner held to his grandmother's belief that he had occult powers. "He will never be of any service as a slave," she said; all his life he pondered that saying.

As he grew to manhood he spent his leisure poring over his Bible, and like the prophets of old withdrew into solitude for fasting and prayer. Once he ran away for this purpose. He gathered about him something like an African Church of his own. It could not have been altogether secret, for his Biblical knowledge, his prophetic insight in interpreting dreams and natural signs and wonders led some white men to consult him.

As a Christian, Turner's faith was very different from that of Sojourner Truth. To her Christ was the living spirit of all embracing, all forgiving lovingkindness; to him Christ was the divinity who had come to bring not peace but a sword.

A holy obsession with blood stood out in everything he thought and did. This perhaps came to him less from his grandmother than from a branch of white man's religion which in these rousing camp meeting days stressed blood above the Beatitudes. The baptism in the river to which he led his followers when they were denied this grace in the white man's church was not only an African rite of purification but a symbol of the mystic baptism in the blood of the Lamb. The symbolic eating of Christ's body and drinking of His blood had overtones of the African mystique of human sacrifice and ritualistic cannibalism. Conjure, Turner specifically denounced, and cannibalism he never advocated. Yet he not a little resembled those mission-bred Africans who would one day join the leopard cult and the Mau Mau. Before his mission on earth was done, he and his followers would solemnly perform the rite of washing their hands in the blood of the white men.

His visions called him to action. In the sky he saw men and

lights "which were the lights of the Savior's hands stretched from east to west, even as they were extended on Calvary for the redemption of sinners." As he labored in the fields he saw drops of blood like dew on the corn, mystic characters on the leaves of the trees, and lines drawn in blood, always blood, resembling the lights he had seen in the sky.

He heard voices. "Seek ye first the kingdom of heaven and all things shall be added unto you," one spirit said to him. Another, having revealed a vision of white spots and black spots in battle, of thunder and lightning, spoke of the task he was born to undertake. "Such is your luck," said this spirit. "Such you are called to see; and let it come rough or smooth, you must surely bear it."

This was a forecast of the action he was destined to take. Now he looked for a sign pointing to the day and the hour. Since childhood he had been a student of the tides, the seasons, the rising of the sun and moon and stars. It was now revealed to him that a solar eclipse was approaching and that this was the divine signal for him to arise "and slay my enemies with their own weapons."

Why, and to what purpose? Unlike Vesey, Turner was to make on the eve of his execution a long and earnest statement, but it concerned mystique only. It contained no intimation of the very practical plans worked out by Vesey and Poyas, or awareness of current events. Had he ever seen a call to rebellion issued in 1829 by David Walker, a Boston Negro, and circulated as far south as Georgia? "Had you rather not be killed than be a slave to that tyrant who takes the life of your mother, wife, and your little children? . . . Believe this, that it is no more harm to kill a man who is trying to kill you than it is for you to take a drink when you are thirsty." If Turner had read that document, he remained mute. His "confession" may have been a more effective instrument of concealment than Vesey's stony silence.

His motive? Far from citing mistreatment, he described

Joseph Travis, whom he had served since 1830, as a kind master. But revolt had been bred into the bone of one whose mother had wanted to strangle him at birth rather than rear him as a slave, and whose grandmother remembered freedom. The slaves of Charleston had been well treated, and except for their conjure man seem to have been singularly untouched by mysticism. Dogs and horses may be reconciled to servitude by kind treatment; cats and men cannot be indefinitely so reconciled. There is a craving for regulating one's own destiny which if unacknowledged results in action.

On the night of August 21, 1831, after a solemn feast celebrated with his followers, Turner and his band set out to execute divine vengeance. They began by slaughtering kind Joseph Travis and his family. Before anyone could give the alarm, 51 whites lay dead, 38 of them women and children. The killing was sacramental; Turner is said to have caused his men to sprinkle each other with the blood of their victims. He himself as priest and prophet killed only when he saw that the blows of his men had been ill directed; then he gave the *coup de grace*. Otherwise he looked on, as he reported, "in silent satisfaction."

To the white men the event was far more terrifying than the Vesey plot, not only because it had actually taken place, but because of its apparent lack of rational motive and systematic planning. Such generalship as that of Poyas would not be met with often; but it required no generalship for a group of slaves to rise spontaneously and do what Turner had done. For a long time few slaveholders in Virginia dared sleep soundly. A cat in the dining room was enough to keep them wakeful for the rest of the night.

Nor was it easier elsewhere in the South. It was especially disturbing that Turner's known confederates who had not been executed had been sold out of the state. No telling where they had got to or what they might do. Kentucky and Mississippi and Georgia slaveholders also rested uneasy, and when at night they heard a sound outside, they flung up a window. "What's that noise? Are the boys all in?"

The "boys" made a private joke of it. The only whites who could were little children who liked to taunt a slave by shouting, "You're an ole Nat Turner! Ole Nat Turner!"

It was given to Turner more than Vesey to affect the course of history. Until 1831 there were still Virginians who declared themselves publicly for emancipation. After the close of the Revolution it had been the fashion for masters to free their slaves by their wills. This tendency had been dying out, and now it ceased altogether except in a very special context. Abolition became a dirty word.

Not many decades earlier John Woolman had succeeded by "gentle persuasion" in turning his co-religionists from slavery; it was largely due to him that Pennsylvania emerged from the Revolution in effect a free state. But it was not written that emancipation was to be achieved in the United States on the pattern set by John Woolman. Slaves were freed in the British West Indies without bloodshed; czarist Russia would find peaceable means to abolish serfdom; even Brazil, which would retain slavery until 1888, was to resolve the problem amicably. But in America, richly endowed in land and treasure, founded on the premise that all men were created equal, it was to be otherwise. Nat Turner's work was admired and presently continued, with something of the same mystique and lack of clear-cut strategy by John Brown at Harpers Ferry; and after Harpers Ferry came Armageddon. Turner's voices had spoken truly; in America freedom was to be purchased only by blood sacrifice.

Even so it was perhaps the white man rather than the African who committed himself to the way of blood. Wherever there were Negro communities fortunate enough to have some degree of autonomy, there were men who sought the road to the future not through violence but through acceptance of civic responsibility performed in cooperation with their fellow citizens.

CHAPTER SIXTEEN

BACK TO AFRICA

THE Free African Society of Philadelphia was still active at the time of Vesey's rebellion. At about the time the Charleston carpenter began discussing his plans with Peter Poyas, in January 1817, it met for a momentous decision.

Two of the founders were present, Absalom Jones and Richard Allen. The former, very old now, and a figure of antique dignity in his frock coat and wig, had long been a semi-official rector at St. Thomas Episcopal Church. He, who as a slave had come by his letters by persuading fellow clerks in his master's store to teach him, lacked in the opinion of the clergymen who examined him the "literary qualifications" for this post, nor was he ever at his best in a pulpit. They let him occupy it because of his moral qualities, "a self-sacrificing spirit," his indefatigable visits to his folk, his "mild and easy manners," and his "consistent religious life."

There had never been doubt about the "literary qualifications" of Richard Allen, who had the advantage of spending his first six years in the Philadelphia household of the distinguished jurist Benjamin Chew, and was collecting a fine library of his own. Now in full charge of the Bethel Church, he was soon to become bishop.

A younger man, James Forten, presided at the meeting in Bethel Church. Unlike the ministers, he had been freeborn; some said there had never been slavery in his family. As owner of a sail loft employing both Negro and white labor, he was the wealthiest Negro in Philadelphia. He had the means to send a son to England for a gentleman's education, was well instructed himself and above all public-spirited.

The subject under consideration was an invitation from a society much younger than theirs; indeed at this date the American Colonization Society, whose president was Bushrod Washington, and whose members were celebrities like Henry Clay and John Randolph, was barely a month old. One of its purposes was to make emancipation possible again even in those states which forbade it. But the Philadelphians' attention was riveted on what was in fact its primary purpose: to rid the South in particular and America at large of the anomalous "third class" of free Negroes ("a dangerous and useless part of the community,") by sending them back to Africa.

Already the young society was about to petition Congress (unsuccessfully) for public funds to transport the slaves, and appeal for contributions from philanthropists north and south. The African Society had before it an invitation to them as freedmen, urging on them the benefit of returning to the homeland and of contributing their mite to support the great venture.

It is improbable that their correspondence included that phrase about the freedmen as being "dangerous and useless." But the words were on record and members of the African Society could read. They considered the invitation, and they rejected it, "with abhorrence."

Philadelphia harbored a few Negroes who remembered

Africa, but this was not characteristic of the Free African Society. The middle term of the name represented no sentimental preoccupation with a mystical homeland; it had been adopted as less liable than "Negro" to odious corruption, and more descriptive than "black." The key word was "free"; the group's orientation was to their future as Americans. The implications of the Colonization Society that they had no such future struck them a body blow.

"Dangerous and useless." Had they been that when at the cost of many of their lives they had served as nurses and burial crew in the yellow fever? Were they that in the War of 1812 when Allen, Jones, and Forten had rallied 2,500 Negroes to work on the defenses of Philadelphia? The Colonization Society was never to live down that undiplomatic phrase, not intended for freedmen to hear, but heard nevertheless. The reply drafted at Bethel Church was typical not only of similar groups at the time but of the more influential Negro convention movement which would come a few years later.

"Whereas our ancestors (not of choice) were the first successful cultivators of the wilds of America, we, their descendants, feel ourselves entitled to participate in the blessings of her luxuriant soil, which their blood and sweat manured; and that any measure . . . having a tendency to banish us from her bosom would not only be cruel but in direct violation of those principles which have been the boast of this republic.

"Resolved, That we never will separate ourselves voluntarily from the slave population in this country; they are our brethren by the ties of consanguinity, of suffering, and of wrong; and we feel that there is more virtue in suffering privations with them, than fancied advantages for a season.

"Resolved, That without arts, without science, without a proper knowledge of government, to cast into the savage wilds of Africa the free people of color, seems to us the circuitous route through which they must return to perpetual bondage.

"Resolved, That having the strongest confidence in the justice of God and philanthropy of the free states, we cheerfully submit our destinies to the guidance of Him who suffers not a sparrow to fall without His special providence."

2.

The back-to-Africa movement had originated in England in 1787 and its purpose had little to do with emancipation. British slavery was then limited to the colonies; all Negroes in England were free, but many were also paupers. Not every freedman had Vassa's ingenuity in making his way in the world; times were hard, and the island had a surfeit of paupers, by no means predominately African. British philanthropists conceived the happy solution of resettling rootless British Negroes in Sierra Leone. In their native clime, on soil where all good things grew with tropical abundance (so Englishmen thought) they would flourish and live happily ever after.

When the first ship set sail for Sierra Leone in 1787 its 411 passengers included sixty white women who had been thoughtfully provided for unmated Africans. They also were paupers, many of them women of ill fame, plucked from the gutters where they were sleeping off their gin. Some had been induced to come aboard at Wapping to be married to selected Africans. These too were befuddled; next morning the wife of the agent, who accompanied her husband on this cruise, heard them asking each other which husband was whose. She busied herself tending the sick and clothing the near naked with what she could spare from her own wardrobe.

It was an extraordinary start for so high-minded an enterprise, but there was precedent. England had always seen its crown colonies as a means of getting rid of its pauper and even its criminal class. It had done so in early Virginia and would continue with Botany Bay. Africans were not the only emigrants to come to America in chains.

Gustavus Vassa served the Sierra Leone project as a purchasing agent. He had left following the sea after a post-Revolutionary voyage to America nearly cost him his freedom and had become an English house servant as a safer way of earning his living. He considered going to Sierra Leone as missionary, but he was too scandalized at corruption in the management to carry out that plan. It was not the transportation of the "wives" that shocked him, but the deals by which inadequate and unwholesome provision was purveyed at inflated prices. For his peace of mind it was well that he never went to Sierra Leone, for it began as a sorry venture.

No attention had been given to the exigencies of life there, perhaps because it was reasoned that Africans required no adjustment, no matter how long they and their ancestors had lived in temperate zones. The settlers arrived in May, in the rainy season, and fell prey to fevers and fluxes. By September there were only 242 of the Negroes left alive and only half the white women. Unable to care for themselves, so many of the former went afield, often to be seized and enslaved at the "factories," that by March 1788 the colony had only 130 survivors of any color.

It was not until 1800 that the colony took root. That was when the transport *Asia* came from Nova Scotia with 550 colonists whose vigorous will to live was a happy contrast to the spiritless and bewildered group from England. On landing they helped the authorities quell an incipient rebellion. Then they planted their allotments, and thanks mostly to them Sierra Leone became a viable colony.

These were the Maroons of Jamaica, who had lived in freedom since 1655 when the British took Jamaica from the Spaniards and many slaves took advantage of the confusion to "maroon" to the mountains. Some Gold Coast Cormantines esconced themselves so soundly that for a century and a half no way was found to dislodge them. They built villages, governed themselves by remembered tribal laws, worshipped the old gods, tilled the land after the ancient fashion.

Unable to oust them, the whites made treaties.

They might have been left permanently in their mountain fastnesses but for two reasons. Their ground being inadequate to provision a growing population, they made periodic raids on the valleys; and their existence was an incentive to rebellion and escape on the part of malcontents on the plantations. During the 1790's, when the British used Cuban bloodhounds to track them down, one body of Maroons finally surrendered. In 1796 they were transported to Nova Scotia and settled near Preston.

This was an act of bad faith on the part of the British; the Maroons had surrendered on a promise that they be allowed to remain in Jamaica, and the principal English negotiator had resigned his commission in protest. Already antagonized when they reached Canada, they were not a success there. Nothing in their experience had prepared them for either land or climate. They fell into rancorous idleness and let the British feed them. Good Nova Scotians looked aghast at their improvidence and their heathen ways, their worship of a deity they called Acompag, and their polygamy. But the newcomers were so touchy, so ready to fight off interference that reforms were impractical. It was a relief when they consented to join the colony in Sierra Leone.

There they built their thatched huts, planted their generous allotments. Used to supporting themselves under far more difficult conditions in Jamaica, they did well. By 1807 they were termed "law-abiding, industrious settlers." They provided a stable nucleus for later émigrés from Britain; the colony was beginning to stand on its own feet, and Sierra Leone was what the American Colonization Society looked to when it formulated its own plans.

Yet even in their new prosperity many Maroons were discontent; for them Jamaica not Africa was the homeland, and some were so stubborn in their importunities that they finally got back. In 1840 when the activities of the American

Colonization Society were in full swing and had resulted in
the founding of Liberia, a reverse migration took place from
their closest neighbor. Slavery having been abolished in the
British West Indies, free Negroes would no longer become an
incentive to slave insurrection; there are still Maroons in
Jamaica. But others remained in Africa, became absorbed
in the indigenous population and were converted to the faith
that was evangelizing the area. This was not one of the Kaffir
religions, nor was it Christianity with its busybody restrictions on family life; it was Islam.

In 1820 and 1821 Sierra Leone gave brief hospitality to
such American Negroes as saw nothing abhorrent in the
proposal that they return to Africa.

3.

In rejecting the invitation to Africa, the Free African Society had not spoken for all Philadelphia Negroes. Slaves in
Maryland and Virginia looking for a means of escape might
equate Philadelphia with "the city called heaven," but those
who got to it found it an unsure refuge.

A new slave trade was in progress. The suppression of
the trade with the Guinea Coast had coincided with the
founding of Alabama, Mississippi, Louisiana, Arkansas, in all
of which planters demanded more labor than was now easily
available. Some Southern proprietors were moving off their
depleted lands to the virgin soil of the west taking their people with them. Others, especially in Virginia, were selling
their surplus field hands. Slave markets and auction blocks
were in business again, but the trade was no longer "genteel." Not only abolitionists deplored the practice; to masters
there was something shocking about selling one's people,
whatever the financial necessity.

Nor did this supply the demand. The old Guinea trade
was being illicitly reopened, the slaves smuggled in through
Cuba. Bands of kidnappers operated even in the north. Phil-

adelphia was a natural hunting ground. Even Richard Allen was once beset by a kidnapper who produced a "warrant" for his arrest as an escaped slave. Luckily for Allen the constable knew him and refused to honor the warrant. For Philadelphia freedmen who were favorably known and whose papers were in order, the city did afford protection.

Life there was, however, far from ideal for those who lacked Forten's working capital or Allen's force of character. Many were more handicapped than Charleston freedmen. When the new class of immigrants, the Irish, the Germans, came to Carolina they were baffled to find that most trades were monopolized by Negroes, slave or free. In Philadelphia they were succeeding in pre-empting such advantages as Negro labor possessed. Not only did they refuse to work with Negro artisans (Forten's sail loft seems to have been an exception), but they resented the assignment of unskilled labor to Negroes. Nor was this a transient condition; times were to get much worse before they got better. There were to be riots, the firing of churches and homes, the mobbing of Negro citizens. One of James Forten's sons would have a narrow escape from a gang.

In 1817 the riots had not started, not in Philadelphia, but the symptoms were apparent. One need not be a prophet to foresee trouble to come.

There were the insults. Could one forget phrases like "vilest of the Negroes," as if all Negroes were vile and the only difference was in degree? Those who had painfully learned their letters wondered if the effort were worth it when they read in a newspaper that the Mississippi legislature was saying that one might as well "confer citizenship on the chimpanzees and ourang outangs" as on Negroes. In Philadelphia they were citizens, but there was a movement to deprive them of the franchise, and presently it would succeed.

If there were really a spot on the planet where they could

be their own masters and the white man forbidden to meddle, what folly not to take advantage of it. Many Negroes, slave and free, took heart from the colonization project. The songs they sang in their churches and hush harbors came to voice a new sentiment.

> "I'm hunting for a city to stay awhile.
> Poor sinner got a home at last."

By the interpretation of one student of Negro spirituals, the city would be Monrovia, and the line "we'll met on Canaan's shore" would refer to Liberia. "Good news, member, good news, I heard from heaven today" would refer to a letter from a Liberian relative.

Some Negroes had been interested in African settlement before the Colonization Society. In 1811 Paul Cuffee, a free Negro of New Bedford, had sailed his own ship to Sierra Leone, and was so favorably impressed that four years later he returned with thirty-eight colonists.

When in 1820 the first group set out for Africa on the *Elizabeth,* more than a third of the eight-six emigrants were from Pennsylvania, and some were from Bethel Church. Indeed their leader, as missionary agent of the Colonization Society, was Daniel Coker, who had preceded Richard Allen as pastor. They were turning their backs on all the Free African Society's hopes for Philadelphia and setting their faces to Africa. They were followed in the spring of 1821 by the *Nautilus* with thirty emigrants and a fresh contingent of agents.

4.

The agents rode cabin class and the immigrants in steerage, doing their own cooking on deck. Elijah Johnson, who would presently be given a responsible post in Africa, rode steerage on the *Elizabeth* and recorded the voyage in his journal.

Like his pastor Coker, he believed it was the migrants'
destiny not only to better themselves but to bring salvation
to Africa. When passengers bickered, he was distressed. "I
think this is a dull lamp for us to carry in the dark land," he
wrote sorrowfully when J. Fisher beat his wife. "In the
place of our coming to do good we do bad," he added when
a pot was thrown overboard in a dispute about cooking.

There was trouble about dogs. E. Wigfall and Peter Small
would not leave for Africa without their pets, and one February day the dogs somehow went overboard. Such was the
desolation in the Wigfall and Small families that the agents
had to come below to comfort them.

There was ostracism. Other passengers would have nothing
to do with one lonely old man. "The people said I was so
dirty that they drove me from one part of the ship to another," he complained to Johnson. Nor would they let him
wash. When he begged for soap they wouldn't give it to
him, and when he helped himself from an open box they
threatened him with a whipping. The old man stood them
off with a knife.

On the Sabbath Coker held service on deck and one day
made a remark recorded without comment by Johnson. "We
will have our church under white men, not under Allen."
It was an odd prediction for a settlement with which white
men were not to meddle, especially as Coker was to become
the first missionary. Perhaps he counted himself as white;
his father had been a slave, but his mother an English indentured servant.

The *Elizabeth* made a good passage with no recorded
deaths beyond the dogs, but Africa was still "the white man's
graveyard," and not the white man's only. By June, twenty-
four of the colonists and three white agents were dead of
fever. They had landed just as the rains were coming on,
and as demoralizing as the fevers was the fact that for more

than a year they had no place to abide. The Colonization Society had expected them to settle on Sherbro Island, to which it believed it had a claim, but Sierra Leone officials dissented. The only concession they would make the new-comers was permission to build temporary shelters near Freetown. Given the high, almost imperial hopes with which they had left America, this was a sorry pass.

The Africans gave them a mixed reception. A local king made a ceremony of welcoming the Negroes but ordered the white men to keep their distance. When a detachment went inland to fetch drinking water, an old man rebuffed them. "Take the same water that brought you here and go back with it."

The outcast on shipboard proved himself hardy and "worked like a horse . . . while younger men were walking about with their hands in their pockets." Coker, in Johnson's opinion, was doling out supplies too grudgingly. He refused the colonists straw hats to wear in the sun, palm oil to light their huts, and in spite of the sickness he limited their rations to salt pork and hard bread. Even the pious Johnson fell out with him.

"Look at your table and chicken coop full, got with the goods that you say were meant for us," he scolded Coker. "You will not give our people a head of tobacco to get clothes with. They have to sell the clothes off their back to buy that which you ought to give them."

So matters stood in the spring of 1821 when the *Nautilus* came, and its agents took action. Abandoning the futile claim to Sherbro Island they scouted along the Grain Coast to Cape Mensurado and got permission from what they called the "aborigines" to settle there. The survivors of the *Elizabeth* were removed with the second lot and set at last to the founding of Liberia.

The *Nautilus* passengers were aggressive; they had demanded their rights on the point of sailing, and once arrived

in Africa declared themselves free of the jurisdiction of
the Colonization Society. When they accused one of their
white agents of mismanaging funds, as Johnson had accused
Coker, the youth was distressed to the point of weeping all
night.

This was Christian Wiltberger, who had connections in
Swedesborough, New Jersey, was very young, very devout,
and also kept a journal. It is a highly subjective document,
reflecting most frequently the author's preoccupation with
the state of his soul and of his bowels; but it also contains
first impressions of Africa. Wiltberger, a recent convert, lost
no time in offering salvation to such Africans as came his
way.

One was a Mandingo who came with bows and arrows
to sell and affably entered into a discussion with Wiltberger
on religion. The Mandingo knew his Koran, and amazed
Wiltberger as a fellowcountrymen had amazed Mungo Park
not long ago with his intimate knowledge of the Old Testament. The agent made no convert, but he did win a friend
who urged him to visit his home. But to the white man Africa
still seemed dark and dangerous and he expressed anxiety
about going so far from base. The Mandingo laughed. "No,
why should I try to kill you?" he said; Wiltberger wrote in
his journal, "I fell in love with the man."

Daily he met the Kroomen, that remarkable coastal people
of the Vai group who for centuries had served white man's
ships as longshoremen. With these Wiltberger's approach
was clumsier, and the laughter he incurred less friendly.

"Oh, your country god no good. He no talk. He no see.
You fall in hole, he no pull you out," was his reply to one
Tom Reed, who was trying to touch him for the wherewith
to buy rum for a funeral in "my country fashion."

One Sunday the new-fledged missionary tried to instruct
a group of Kroomen, and having found that they "no sabby
either God's day or God's book" pronounced judgment: "You

got bad heart."

"No," said a spokesman. "I no got bad heart."

The company sat companionably about the customary fire. Looking into its flames Wiltberger saw an opportunity to demonstrate the reality of hell. First he asked one man to touch a finger to the flame and then preached what was surely one of the least comprehensible sermons ever uttered in Africa: "When your body die, he go into ground, but you got something inside you, he no die. He He put in fire; he always stay there."

The flame-toucher must have lost himself trying to unscramble the he-he's. He said, "Well, all one," and then laughed, and a howl of laughter that broke up the meeting came from his friends. Wiltberger retired to note in his journal that no one had ever converted a Krooman.

But when he offered them a reading lesson, he found them attentive. The Kroomen were above all things practical; at about this time one of them was engaging in the same experiment that the Cherokee Sequoia was currently undertaking in America, the invention of a syllabary, so that "natives," Cherokee or Vai, could write their own language without waiting for the white man to teach them English. Neither project had been completed at this date, and Wiltberger was pleasantly surprised at the absorption with which they followed his efforts to teach them to "sabby book" and the docility with which they presently knelt with him in prayer.

5.

As a Zionist movement, the work of the American Colonization Society aroused more sentiment among whites than among "Africans." Too few of the latter by this time had any connection with the homeland, and even if they did, Liberia was almost nobody's Zion. The provenance of the American Negro had been the whole Guinea Coast, Congo,

Angola, and to some extent Mozambique and Madagascar; if a literal attempt had been made to return each to his ancestral Zion, the enterprise could have bankrupted the United States Treasury. Few Afro-Americans had done any reading on Africa, an exception being the eminent Frederick Douglass, who found in one account what seemed to be a portrait of the mother he had last seen when he was six. When Liberia took root and became a nation, it did arouse interest, but it was more practical than sentimental.

But sentiment was strong among the white men. Campaigns for funds brought generous response, and branches of the Society sprang up both north and south, especially in Maryland and Virginia. The one form of emancipation that the South could accept had been discovered. There the abolition movement had come to a dead halt after Nat Turner's rebellion, but there were still masters who longed to confer the benefits of freedom on their people.

Such white fathers of slaves as felt an obligation toward mistress and offspring had been placed in an impossible position by the black codes. Sending their mulatto children north to be educated and live as freedmen required more fortune than every paterfamilias possessed and also deprived them of affectionate companionship. South Carolina had a remarkable case of a man in this quandary.

He was Elijah Willis of Barnwell, who had taken his slave Amy as consort and brought up in his household not only her five children by him but three by her previous husband, a slave. Visitors to his home saw him sit at table with his youngest in his lap, petting it, giving it choice morsels from his plate, or calling in field hands to make little wagons for the elder children. There were few visitors, for though it was common enough for a white man to have a slave mistress, flaunting the situation as Willis did was an affront to society.

Intimations of mortality interrupted his family happiness.

Willis had made a will providing that his estate be sold on his death and the proceeds applied to settling Amy and her children in a free state. But he could not count on its being honored in South Carolina, especially as he had nephews who counted on the inheritance and barely kept their derision under control in his presence.

When he developed a "disposition to apoplexy" and knew that time was running out, he loaded his family on an "upward" train, and ill as he was, set out with them for Cincinnati. At Louisville the party transferred to an Ohio River steamer; at Cincinnati they disembarked. A hackney was waiting; Willis made a start for it, but he had spent his last strength. He collapsed and died on the wharf; they buried him in the Negro cemetery.

The nephews contested the will with every chance of success. Under South Carolina law a slave could not inherit; under Federal law—the Fugitive Slave Act—the arrival at Cincinnati did not necessarily free Amy and her children. One jury voided the will, but the judge refused to accept their verdict that Willis was insane and ordered a new trial before the South Carolina Supreme Court.

This time the heroic purpose of Willis prevailed. Judge C. J. O'Neall, author of many interesting rulings in such matters, put the case for the majority. "They were free from the moment when, by the consent of their master, they were placed upon the soil of Ohio to be free. I have no idea that the soil of Ohio *per se* confers freedom. It is the act of the master which has that effect. . . . To permit the devise in their favor to operate is, we are told, contrary to the policy of South Carolina. But I should feel myself degraded if like some in Ohio and other abolitionist states I trampled on law and constitution in obedience to the popular will. There is no law in South Carolina which declares that the trusts in their favor are void."

Willis had never considered sending his family to Africa;

it might have seemed to him a barbarous fate for those he loved. But his plight was, in extreme degree, that of many Southerners who against all law and precedent wanted their people to be free.

There were owners willing to impoverish themselves, not only by sending in the persons of their slaves the most valuable part of their property, but by mortgaging what they had left so that their people could go well provided to their new homes. They worried about the hazards. "Pray ask that he may be cared for during the fever," one woman wrote in entrusting a man to the Society. "If he were to die, I should feel a heavy responsibility on me."

Often the matter was arranged in the master's will, sometimes with the provision that the slaves were to have an option. One such beneficiary chose Liberia, and not liking what he saw when he got there came back on the same ship. He supposed that the act of making the voyage had set him free; the will had stipulated going to Liberia, but had said not a word about staying there. But the court to which the case was referred did not agree, and Sam Martin returned to slavery in Kentucky.

An occasional master foisted his slaves on the Society for embarrassing personal reasons, like the North Carolina widower whose intended would not marry him until he exported his concubine and mulatto children.

John McDonough, owner of a large estate in Louisiana, was one of the most munificent contributors. With him, emancipation was not a gift outright; he made his slaves work for it by designating hours when they could work for pay. There was twofold wisdom in this: he could confer freedom without beggaring himself, and the laborer in the meantime acquired sound habits of industry and self-help that would serve him well as a freedman. When a laborer had paid his price, much of his family was permitted to accompany him to Liberia. By 1842 McDonough had a group of eighty, fifty-five adults and their children, ready for the journey. He equipped them with tools, clothing, provision, and by special permission from the Louisiana legislature he had already given them "a good English education." He was not sending his misfits, but his most responsible and best trained workers.

His will provided for the transportation of all the rest and a bequest to the Colonization Society of $25,000 a year. His testament concluded with an address to the American freedmen. "Having been a friend of the black and colored man all through my long life, I will now give them . . . a parting counsel that they may separate themselves from the white man and depart to the land of their fathers, where they and their posterity may be safe, may be happy, having nothing to make them afraid."

His sentiments were echoed in the new Liberian Constitution, which debarred white men from citizenship and adopted the motto, "The love of liberty brought us here." The Liberian Declaration of Independence contained a commentary on the American experience: "We were everywhere shut out from all civil office. We were excluded from all participation in the government. We were taxed without our consent. . . . We were made a separate and distinct class, and against us every avenue of improvement was effectually closed. Strangers from other lands of a color different from ours were preferred before us."

But even during the founding of the new nation, where in contrast to Sierra Leone the newcomers took over the control from the "aborigines" already on the spot, American free Negroes at large were not disposed to follow and share these advantages. Americans they were, in spite of all temptations to belong to other nations; Americans they were determined to remain. The problem lay in getting fellow Americans to recognize them for what they were.

CHAPTER SEVENTEEN

THE BATTLE
FOR AMERICA

T HE OLD Free African Society had not long survived its rejection of the invitation to Africa. Its activities were absorbed by the Negro churches to which it had given birth and which in turn gave rise to the first of a series of Negro conventions.

The churches had grown out of an incident in November 1787 when St. George's Methodist, to which both Richard Allen and Absalom Jones belonged, relegated its Negro members to the gallery. Met at the door with these orders, the Negroes had complied; during worship, while Jones knelt in prayer, a trustee interrupted with directions to move farther back.

"Wait only until prayer is over, and I will get up and trouble you no more," replied Jones, gentlest of men. The prayer completed, he and his companions rose from their knees, and "they were no more plagued with us in that church."

Discussion of the incident in the African Society led to a resolution to found a church where Negroes could worship free of such humiliation. Allen had already been giving religious instruction to Negro groups at five in the morning and in the evening; these now became the nucleus of Bethel Methodist, whose first sanctuary was a blacksmith shop. But some parishioners at St. George's were so wroth with the Methodists they became Episcopalians and founded St. Thomas.

The fact that the new congregations were in effect practicing self-segregation drew protests from both whites and Negroes. Some of the latter held that it was better to work and worship with the whites, whatever the incidental irritations. Some white ministers considered the Negroes to be motivated by petty vanity. One justified the discrimination at St. George's, saying that it was "a signal error to break down every barrier which instinctive nature has reared in the path of free intercourse."

Nevertheless both congregations had their way. Bishop Francis Asbury dedicated Bethel; Allen was allowed to preach and later ordained. Congregations at St. Thomas had to listen to white rectors. "You are a people who have walked in darkness, unacquainted with divine revelation and the covenant of grace in your own country," Dr. Samuel Magaw of St. Paul's told them. "Your fathers and perhaps some of you now present did, near the shores of the Senegal and the Gambia . . . or maybe in Benin, Congo, and Angola" practice idolatry and "dancing in wild circles, mutter to devils, or in affrighted gaze, yell to the pale moon to save you."

Dr. Magaw was a kind friend who had never permitted segregation in his own church; his discourse was educational, especially for the many who knew nothing of Africa. But they craved to hear something more to the point than the alleged misdeeds of almost mythical ancestors. They pleaded for a pastor of their own color, and presently Absalom Jones occupied the pulpit.

He was long dead and Bishop Allen within months of the close of his life when in November 1830 a group met in Bethel Church to consider the summoning of a national Negro convention. The preliminary convention might have been confined to the membership of Bethel but for an invasion of half a dozen "grave, stern-looking men" who came from Zion Methodist to demand by what authority Bethel arrogated to itself the right to represent the colored people at large. The augmented group laid the plans for the First National Negro Convention, which met in Philadelphia in June 1831.

The date was more significant than they knew. In Virginia, Nat Turner, whose aims as much resembled theirs as his methods differed, was searching the Bible and the skies for the divine signal for action. In Philadelphia the convention brought together delegates from Virginia to Rhode Island, who represented a new generation of leaders. Of the old Free African Society only James Forten now survived.

They were dedicated to asserting the Negro's right to American citizenship. Like the four succeeding conventions, one of which met in New York, they denounced the American Colonization Society, though one colony received their qualified support: a small settlement in Ontario founded by fugitive slaves for whom Ohio had become an uneasy sanctuary. The 1831 convention recommended that the Colonization Society divert its resources to this enterprise "where it can complete much with less means and more convenience and in a climate more congenial to the health and prosperity of its colonists."

All emphasis was placed on the Negroes' improving themselves where they were, on attaining recognition as Americans. To this end they were urged to "abandon the use of the word colored when either speaking or writing about themselves, and especially to remove the title of African from their institutions and the marbles of their churches." A fund was started to found a Negro trade school; steadfast endeavor was urged on the freedmen.

"It is with us to say whether [we] shall assume a rank and standing among the nations of the earth as men. . . . By a brother's love, and by all that makes man dear to men, awake in time! Be wise! Be free! Endeavor to walk with circumspection, be obedient to the laws of our common country; honor and respect its lawmakers and lawgivers, and through all, let us not forget to respect ourselves."

After 1835 this phase of the convention movement lapsed. Had there been too much discouragement? An attempt to found a Negro trade school in New Haven had been thwarted by New Haven's violent refusal to have any part in it. The legislature of Pennsylvania was preparing to renounce the generosity by which its slaves had been given not only their freedom but the franchise.

Yet the Negroes' fight for recognition as Americans went on, continued in Philadelphia by the self-improvement societies established in the spirit of old Ben Franklin, by the churches, and by individuals. The Banneker Society exposed "the hollow-heartedness of American liberty" by proclaiming August 1 as the Negro independence day, in honor of emancipation in the British colonies. It was observed at Spring Mills, "a romantic region" on the Schuylkill, to which they ran excursion trains to give their members access to the boating, picnic grounds, band concerts, and oratory.

As the Free African leaders grew old and died, a new generation took their place. Bishop Allen was succeeded by that pastor of Charleston's African Church whose role in Vesey's rebellion had been so ambiguous, Morris Brown; James Forten by his sons. Also from Charleston came a very important leader, Robert Purvis.

It is possible that rumors of "something serious about to take place" had impelled William Purvis to remove his three sons from Charleston in 1820, when Robert was ten. As of that date Vesey's plans were well advanced and the Purvis boys may have picked up some inkling of them. The ability of children to run about without rousing suspicion makes them first class spies; among the witnesses of the Vesey affair was a lad of Robert's age who had overheard bits of conversation that became significant in retrospect.

The elder Purvis, an Englishman who had been a cotton broker in Charleston, had good reasons for not wanting to get caught in what was impending. He was also impelled by the circumstances that drove Elijah Willis to Ohio; the mother of his sons was an African. She was Dido Badaraska, kidnapped in Morocco as a twelve-year-old, taken to the coast on a camel, and sent to South Carolina. There she found favor with "a wealthy maiden lady," who gave her freedom and an annuity of $60. She was a free woman of color when Purvis met her, and their children were freeborn.

But there was no future for them in Charleston. Purvis could not even be sure the children would inherit his substantial property, for under local law they must have been technically illegitimate. It was his purpose to remove them to England, but he got no farther than Philadelphia, where he died.

There young Robert grew up, and when he was of age, threw himself into the convention movement, into founding a Philadelphia anti-slavery society, into fighting the disenfranchisement of the Negro, into all the details of the battle for America.

All this he did of his own election, for had he chosen he could have "passed" and so ridded himself of any part of the Negro problem. Physically he favored his father more than his mother, and she herself, as a Moor, was probably of a Hamitic or Caucasoid strain. Uncounted thousands of mixed bloods had joined the white community by leaving family and friends and going where they were not known. But that was not the way of young Purvis. He declared himself a Negro as he declared himself an American. "We are Pennsylvanians," he wrote in 1838, "and we hope to see the day when Pennsylvania will . . . be proud of us, as she now has no reason to be ashamed."

Under the influence of William Lloyd Garrison he became a militant abolitionist, made his fine home in the Philadelphia suburbs a way station on the underground railroad, and became known as a radical. Still in his early twenties at the time of Nat Turner's rebellion, he and his kind were accused of fomenting it, and Pennsylvania considered closing its borders to fugitive slaves. In collaboration with James Forten and William Phippin, Purvis wrote an eloquent disclaimer.

"Who can turn to the page in . . . history which exhibits a single instance of insurrection or violation of the peace of society resulting from the residence of a colored population in this commonwealth?" it asked. "As children of the state [we] look to it as guardian and protector, and in common with you feel the necessity of maintaining law and order for the protection of the commonweal."

This statement answered not only the specific accusation but the American Colonization Society's claim that free Negroes were a useless and dangerous element. The authors appended a statistical document to demonstrate that, in proportion to their numbers in Philadelphia, Negroes did not predominate among those on poor relief, that benevolent societies took care of their own, and that in spite of the limited opportunities to educate their children and apprentice their youth to the trades, the city had 500 Negro artisans, most of whom owned property and paid taxes.

When Pennsylvania rescinded the Negro franchise, Purvis joined two of Forten's sons and Bishop Brown in a protest.

They cited the hallowed revolutionary argument that taxation without representation is tyranny, and continued, "It is the safeguard of the strongest that he lives under a government which is obliged to respect the voice of the weakest. When you have taken from an individual his right to vote, you have made the government in regard to him a mere despotism, and you have taken a step towards making it a despotism to all. . . . We love our native country, much as it has wronged us, and in the peaceable exercise of our inalienable rights we will cling to it. . . . Will you starve our patriotism?"

It was a long, well-reasoned, carefully documented protest, but it was in vain. Pennsylvania duly marked its voting booth, "For Whites Only."

Later came a more stunning blow, the bitterest in the history of American slavery, the Dred Scott decision. At last the controversy about Jefferson's "inalienable rights" was settled; the highest authority in the land denied that they could be applied to Africans imported as slaves, or to their descendants, whether slave or free. Under no circumstance could United States citizenship be conferred on a Negro.

Yet one Negro had proof of American citizenship; Purvis had obtained a passport without disguising his Negro origin. It had taken doing; at first the State Department had sent him only an "informal ticket of leave," which he would not accept. His protest came to the attention of President Andrew Jackson who had ordered the passport issued him in due form.

Long before then, Purvis's handsome goatee had become as familiar a mark of distinction as Absalom Jones's frock coat and wig, and he was as forceful a speaker as Richard Allen. "I think I have never seen a finer face and figure," wrote John Greenleaf Whittier, "and his manner, words, and bearing are in keeping."

On the national stage his fame was second only to that of

Frederick Douglass. Like Purvis, Douglass had a white father, but the circumstances were different. The union with his mother, the Maryland slave Harriet Bailey, had been casual and brought no advantage to either mother or son. In 1838, the year when Pennsylvania abolished Negro civil rights, Douglass escaped to New England, and after harsh beginnings as a day laborer, became a prime figure in the Abolition movement.

He had a tremendous advantage over Purvis, whose knowledge of slavery, like the white man's, derived from observation and hearsay. Douglass knew every detail of the experience this side of transportation from Africa, from the hunger of a child hanging like a puppy about the Great House, hopeful of scraps, to labor in both house and field. His superb gift for expression, the richness of his memory of human incident, his insights into patterns of behavior of both slave and master made him a peerless speaker, and his autobiography became a classic.

He and Purvis fought on national fronts for the same ends, but sometimes the ex-slave, who had risen the hard way, resented the eminence of the "voluntary Negro," who had had the rare experience of being born with a silver spoon in his mouth. "Blood-soaked riches," remarked Douglass of the spoon. It was unfair, and untrue except in the broad sense that as a cotton broker the elder Purvis had necessarily dealt in the products of slave labor.

Both men lived into the 1890's and saw revolutionary change. They saw emancipation come, not in the spirit of gentle persuasion with which John Woolman had worked for it, but in Nat Turner's vision and practice, by the way of blood. John Brown, who admired Turner, struck the first blow, and then most bloodily came the Civil War.

Purvis could not know the stress of spirit in which Lincoln, seeking privacy in a telegraph office, worked out the first draft of his Emancipation Proclamation, but he knew

that Lincoln hoped to colonize the freedmen. The President
had discussed the matter with freedmen of the District of
Columbia, offering them not little Liberia alone, but Central
America. What did Lincoln fear, that Negroes could not be
Americans or that their fellow Americans wouldn't let
them? His suggestion evoked no enthusiasm, and when he
signed the proclamation, it contained no reference to colonization. The freedmen were Americans.

Purvis saw citizenship achieved during Reconstruction,
when Negroes sat in Southern legislatures; then he saw the
reversal when the Ku Klux Klan rode to drive the freedmen
back to what was deemed "their place." Rich man's son
though he was, he had some conception of the odds against
which the freedmen struggled, most of them illiterate, trained
only for slave labor and without a foot of land to call their
own. There had been a dream that each would receive forty
acres and a mule; czarist Russia had given its liberated serfs
something like that. But it was a brief dream, considered
naive by their mentors. Some would drift into the approxi-
mate slavery of the sharecropper in debt to the company
store.

The end of slavery was only the beginning of the real
battle for America.

2.

And the battle for America would be long and hard,
marked by heart-breaking reverses. Had the likes of Absalom
Jones and Bishop Allen foreseen how long and how hard it
would be they might conceivably have recommended a
mass exodus to Liberia.

Yet how could they foresee so much? Were not those who
had bought their freedom in the same situation as the white
indentured servants who had also undergone years of servitude before they became their own masters? Such of the
latter as were industrious and blessed with good fortune

had become respected members of their community, elected to high office by neighbors who had forgotten their humble beginnings; their children might never know that they had once labored in the fields with slaves.

Nor were Africans the only immigrants whose habitation had been enforced. Even colonial New England, where slavery had never been important, had Scotch prisoners of war transported to hard labor. Many early settlers in the South had been convicts, paupers, slum children, kidnapped as ruthlessly as Vassa had been. There had been little difference between the condition of these and that of the Africans. Yet their children were free, and if they made their way in the world, the servitude of their fathers was not held a reproach to them.

The horrors of the Middle Passage were sometimes matched and even exceeded by the horrors of the newer immigrant ships. The latter less resembled floating concentration camps in that the passengers were not chained, but they were almost as tightly stowed, and were always given less care than a responsible captain on a slaver gave his human cargo. The master had no interest in them beyond collecting their fare. If they had insufficient clothing against the cold, if their provisions ran out, they must make what shift they could. When they fell ill, there was no medical attendance for them, nor were sailors sent to clean their quarters. Pestilence and starvation were often the lot of the passengers.

In the new country they had to find their way. Those newcomers who in Philadelphia as elsewhere had pressed the free Negroes for even the most menial jobs were driven by brute necessity. They too suffered contumely from the established population, were mocked as "shanty Irish," "micks," "dumb Dutchmen." Yet after harsh beginnings they too would rise in the world.

Then why not also the free Negroes? Some did. But for

them the task was triply difficult and there were always those who couldn't make it at all. The difference lay in what Southern judges called "the badge of servitude," the color of their skins. No one looking at the children of an Irish or German immigrant could tell what their fathers had been. With the children of a Negro an onlooker could take in everything at a glance. It was the circumstance that had imposed slavery on the African in the first place, the high visibility that prevented a Negro fugitive from blending into the population as a white fugitive could do.

Afro-Americans were losing some African physical characteristics, and not by racial mixture only. Observers in the West Indies had noticed that even in the lifetime of an individual African his features underwent perceptible change; a flat nose, for instance, sometimes took a sharper definition. Something in the environment was effecting a gradual change, even to some degree in pigmentation. The settlers of Liberia quite rightly, if sometimes too bumptiously, held themselves a different breed from the "aborigines." But no change, unless hastened by racial blending, obliterated the difference.

If America had been a different place, committed to rigid stratification, to absolutist rule, the freedmen might have docilely accepted an inferior position, as in fact some individuals seemed content to do. But America was not that sort of place. Social mobility had been in the air from the first; the whole colonial history had been a struggle by the settlers to regulate their own destinies without dictation from overseas. It had culminated in the American Revolution and in the new way of life formulated in the daring preamble to the Declaration of Independence. The freedmen, no matter how carefully they were barred from Fourth of July celebrations, had heard it. Those who declined the invitation to Africa set out to make a practical application of those self-evident truths that all men were created equal and that their inalienable rights included life, liberty, and the pursuit of happiness.

The long struggle in which they engaged was a battle by Americans, of Americans, and for Americans. It may be the highest tribute that America has received from any of us immigrants that these remained of their own will in a country that tried to reject them, and that they refused stubbornly to accept less than the promises of the Declaration.

NOTES

THE AFRICAN BACKGROUND (Chaps. I–V)

Mungo Park is my principal authority for Chapters II-IV. I drew on his *Travels in the Interior Districts of Africa . . . in the years 1795, 1796, 1797* (London, 1816), and also, though this volume is less relevant, his *Journal of a Mission to the Interior of Africa in the Year 1805* (Philadelphia, 1815). Chapter V is based on Gustavus Vassa's *The Life of Olaudah Equiano or Gustavus Vassa, the African. Written by Himself* (Boston, 1837). The Schonberg Collection of the New York Public Library also contains a typescript of a master's thesis by Augusta Juanita Johnson, *An Introduction to the Autobiography of Gustavus Vassa* (Atlanta University, 1936).

Other personal accounts of African life in this period:

Canot, Capt. Theodore, Malcolm Cowley, ed. *Adventures of an African Slaver* (New York, 1928).

Hawkins, Joseph. *Voyage to the Coast of Africa* (Philadelphia, 1797).

Owen, Nicholas. *Journal of a Slave Dealer,* Evaline Martin, ed. (London, 1930).

Some general sources of West African background:

Basden, George Thomas. *Niger Ibos* (London, 1938).

Church, R. J. Harrison. *West Africa* (London, 1957).

Davidson, Basil. *Black Mother* (Boston, 1961).

——. *The Lost Cities of Africa* (Boston, 1959).

Fage, J. D. *An Introduction to the History of West Africa* (Cambridge, 1955).

Herskovitz, Melville J. *Dahomey and the Ancient West African Kingdom,* 2 vols. (New York, 1938).

Ritner, Peter. *The Death of Africa* (New York, 1960).

Schiffers, Heinrich. *The Quest for Africa* (New York, 1957).

Seligman, C. G. *Races of Africa* (London, 1930).

THE SLAVERS AND THE SLAVE MARKET
(Chaps. VI, VII)

THE CHAPTER called "Immigrant Ship" is based on Vassa's narrative and the account of the voyage of the *Duke of Argyle* as recorded in Bernard Martin's *John Newton* (London, 1950). Other details are from Volume II of the most massive documentary collection on the subject: Elizabeth Donnan's *Documents Illustrative of the History of the Slave Trade to America*, 5 vols. (Washington, D.C., 1930–1935). A standard reference on this subject is George Francis Dow's *Slave Ships and Slavery* (Salem, 1927); the most recent and one of the best is by Daniel P. Mannix in collaboration with Malcolm Cowley, *Black Cargoes* (New York, 1962).

The description of the slave market is drawn from Vassa and the correspondence of Henry Laurens as printed in Donnan IV, and his manuscript letter books in the South Carolina Historical Society in Charleston. I also drew some material from "Professional Planter" (Dr. H. Collins), *Practical Rules for the Management and Medical Treatment of Negro Slaves in the Sugar Colonies* (London, 1811) and a diary by Sir William Young included in Bryan Edwards' *History of the West Indies* (London, 1807).

THE SEASONING (Chap. VIII)

THE VITAL period of the "seasoning" and the beginning of the acculturation of the newly arrived Africans has been the least studied. Even the best standard histories give only fragmentary accounts. Herskovitz attacks the subject in his *Myth of the Negro Past* (New York, 1941), but his research is more anthropological than historical. My chapter represents an intricate mosaic of sources, of which I shall identify only the most important.

I am grateful for Vassa's intimately personal account, which is supplemented by the other authentic account of a transplanted slave, that of Venture Smith, available in the Connecticut Historical Society in Hartford. The documents cited in connection with the later chapters on Vesey's Rebellion also contain personal material.

Otherwise my most valuable sources are "Professional Planter" and the extraordinary collection of direct observations of the first years of the transplanted Africans in the two volumes of depositions in Great Britain, *The State of the West India Colonies, Report from a Select*

Committee of the House of Lords (London, 1832).

Though I made no direct use of this source, there are illuminating sidelights of this phase in Donald Pierson's, *Negroes in Brazil, A Study of Race Contacts at Bahia* (Chicago, 1942).

Francis Le Jau's observations of South Carolina are drawn from Roll I of the microfilm of the records of the Society of the Propagation of the Gospel, which I studied at the South Carolina Archives in Columbia. A variety of material came from Helen T. Catterall's *Judicial Cases Concerning American Slavery and the Negro,* 5 vols. (Washington, D.C., 1926–1937). Material used in this chapter was drawn from Volumes I, II.

PROBLEMS OF THE FREEDMEN (Chap. IX, X)

MATERIAL in Chapter IX is drawn from the narratives of Gustavus Vassa, Venture Smith, the House of Lords Select Committee, and Catterall's *Judicial Cases.* Volume I of the later contains depositions of Indian ancestry by Virginia slaves and the famous case of George Wythe.

Accounts of the community of free Negroes in Philadelphia are found in the following:

Douglass, Rev. William. *Annals of the First African Church in the U.S.A.* (Philadelphia, 1862).

Bardolph, Richard. *The Negro Vanguard* (New York, 1959).

Turner, Edward Raymond, *The Negro in Pennsylvania, 1639–1861* (Washington, D.C., 1911).

Wesley, Charles H. *Richard Allen, Apostle of Freedom* (Washington, D.C., 1935).

The story of the yellow fever is drawn from the personal narratives of the principals:

Jones, Absalom and Richard Allen. *A Narrative of the Proceedings of the Black People During the Late Awful Calamity in Philadelphia in the Year 1793 and a Refutation of Some Censures* (Philadelphia, 1794).

Rush, Benjamin. *An Account of the Bilious Yellow Fever as it Appeared in the City of Philadelphia in the Year 1793* (Philadelphia, 1794).

THE END OF THE SLAVE TRADE THROUGH
VESEY'S AND TURNER'S REBELLIONS
(Chaps. XI–XV)

THE ACCOUNT of the end of the legal slave trade is largely based on
Donnan, IV. In addition to Mannix and Cowley's *Black Cargoes,* a
standard scholarly source is W. E. Burghardt DuBois, *The Suppression of the African Slave Trade to the U.S.A., 1638–1870* (New York,
1896).

The details of Vesey's Rebellion and the background of the partici-
pants, are drawn primarily from two sources:

> Corporation of Charleston. *An Account of the Late Intended
> Insurrection by a Portion of the Blacks in This City* (Charleston,
> 1822).
>
> Kennedy, Lionel H. and Thomas Parker. *An Official Report of
> the Trials of Sundry Negroes Charged with an Attempt to
> Raise an Insurrection* (Charleston, 1822).

The episode is also described in the following:

> Aptheker, Herbert, ed. *A Documentary History of the Negro
> People in the United States* (New York, 1951).
>
> ———. *Negro Slave Revolts in the United States* (New York,
> 1939).
>
> Carroll, Joseph Cephas. *Slave Insurrection in the United States,
> 1800–1865* (Boston, 1938).
>
> Grimké, Archibald H. *Right on the Scaffold, or The Martyrs of
> 1822,* American Negro Academy Occasional Paper No. 7
> (Washington, D.C., 1901).
>
> Higginson, H. L. "Denmark Vesey," *The Atlantic Monthly,* June,
> 1861.

Material on Nat Turner is available in the volumes by Aptheker
and Carroll, and in *The Confession of Nat Turner, the Leader of the
Late Insurrection in Southampton, as fully and voluntarily made to
Thomas R. Gray* (Richmond, 1832). The Virginia State Archives in
Richmond contain forty boxes on the subject under the heading of
The Southampton Insurrection.

The story of Sojourner Truth is drawn from Arthur Huff Fausset's
Sojourner Truth, God's Faithful Pilgrim (Chapel Hill, 1938), and
from Mrs. Francis W. Titus's *Narrative of Sojourner Truth, a Northern
Slave* (Battle Creek, Mich., 1860).

THE BACK TO AFRICA MOVEMENT (Chap. XVI)

THE SIERRA LEONE episode gets some attention from Vassa, and is more fully described in:
>Archibald, A. G. "Story of the Deportation of Negroes from Nova Scotia to Sierra Leone," Nova Scotia Historical Society *Collections*, VII, 1889–91.
>Crooks, J. J. *A History of the Colony of Sierra Leone Western Africa* (London, 1903).

The journals of Elijah Johnson and Christian Wiltberger are in the manuscript collection of the Library of Congress. A printed firsthand account of Liberia, as of 1836, is David Francis, *Wanderings on the Seas and Shores of Africa* (New York, 1843).

The activities of the Colonization Society are given a scholarly review by Earl Lee Fox in *The American Colonization Society, 1817–1840* (Baltimore, 1919).

John McDonough's will is in Catterall III, 628–30. The theory of the origin of the spirituals is from Miles Mark Fisher's *Negro Slave Songs in the United States* (Ithaca, N.Y., 1953).

Details on the Negro Convention movement are in Aptheker's *Documentary History*. The Pennsylvania Historical Society in Philadelphia has a vast miscellany of material on societies and churches in Philadelphia, including portraits of Absalom Jones and Richard Allen, and a typescript of biographical detail on William Purvis and James Forten.

SUPPLEMENTARY READING LIST
Documents, Diaries, Personal Accounts

Abdy, E. S. *Journal of a Residence and Tour in the U.S.A. from April, 1833 to October, 1834* (London, 1835).
Asbury, Francis. *The Journal of the Rev. Francis Asbury, Bishop of the Methodist Episcopal Church* (New York, 1852).
Ball, Charles. *Fifty Years in Chains, or the Life of an American Slave* (Indianapolis, 1853).
Bassett, John Spencer. *The Southern Plantation Overseer as Revealed in his Letters* (Northampton, Mass., 1925).
Douglass, Frederick. *Life and Times* (Hartford, 1883).
Fithian, Philip Vickers. *Journal and Letters, 1773–1774. A Plantation Tutor of the Old Dominion.* Edited by Hunter Dickinson Farish

(Williamsburg, Va., 1943).

Kemble, Frances Anne. *Journal of a Residence on a Georgian Plantation in 1838–1839* (New York, 1863).

Northrup, Solomon. *Twelve Years a Slave* (Buffalo, 1853).

Olmsted, Frederick L. *A Journey in the Back Country* (New York, 1860).

————. *Journeys and Exploration in the Cotton Kingdom* (London, 1861).

Ransom, William and Edwin Adams Davis, editors. *William Johnson's Nachez, the Ante-Bellum Diary of a Free Negro* (Louisiana University, 1951).

Woolman, John. *Journal.* Janet Whitney ed. (Chicago, 1950).

General

Bennett, Lerone, Jr. *Before the Mayflower: A History of the Negro in America 1619–1962* (Chicago, 1962).

Butcher, Margaret Just. *The Negro in American Culture.* Based on materials collected by Alain Leroy Locke (New York, 1956).

Franklin, John Hope. *From Slavery to Freedom.* A History of American Negroes (New York, 1947).

Frazier, E. Franklin. *The Negro Family in the United States* (Chicago, 1939).

————. *The Negro in the United States* (New York, 1949).

Furnas, J. C. *Goodbye to Uncle Tom* (New York, 1956).

Hughes, Langston and Milton Meltzer. *A Pictorial History of the Negro in America* (New York, 1956).

Nieboer, H. J. *Slavery as an Industrial System.* Ethnological Institute (The Hague, 1900).

Phillips, Ulrich Bonnell. *American Negro Slavery* (New York, 1952).

————. *Life and Labor in the Old South* (Boston, 1929).

Redding, Saunders. *The Lonesome Road* (New York, 1958).

————. *They Came in Chains* (New York, 1950).

Stampp, Kenneth M. *The Peculiar Institution* (New York, 1956).

WPA. *The Negro in Virginia* (Hampton Institute, Va., 1940).